KIDS STUFF
FRENCH

KIDS STUFF FRENCH

Easy French Phrases for You and Your Kids

Therese Slevin Pirz

BILINGUAL KIDS SERIES

CHOU CHOU PRESS
P.O. BOX 152
SHOREHAM, N.Y. 11786
www.bilingualkids.com

Copyright c 2000 by Therese Slevin Pirz

All rights reserved. No part of this book may be produced or utilized in any form or by any means, electronic or mechanical, including photocopying, recording or by any information storage or retrieval system without permission in writing from the publisher.

Printed in the United States of America

First Edition.
Library of Congress Catalog Card No. 00-90331

ISBN   0-9606140-5-2

Order direct from the publisher:

        Chou Chou Press
        P.O. Box 152
        Shoreham, N.Y. 11786
        www.bilingualkids.com

To all Mothers —
 Blessed Mother,
  Mom,
   Family, Friends and Neighbors —

CONTENTS
ACKNOWLEDGMENTS
PREFACE

SALUTATIONS	GREETINGS	13
La SALLE de BAINS	BATHROOM	17
S'HABILLER	GETTING DRESSED	22
L'HEURE du REPAS	MEALTIME	25
CONVERSATIONS	CONVERSATIONS	31
AIDER chez TOI	HELPING at HOME	53
Les CLASSES chez TOI	SCHOOL at HOME	60
La LOUANGE	PRAISE	66
FAIRE des COURSES	SHOPPING	69
S'AMUSER !	FUN !	73
SAMEDI APRÈS-MIDI	SATURDAY AFTERNOON	91
Les EXCLAMATIONS	EXCLAMATIONS	100
La FÊTE d'ANNIVERSAIRE	BIRTHDAY PARTY	109
L'HEURE du COUCHER	BEDTIME	111
Le TEMPS	WEATHER	116
L'HEURE	TIME	121
QUANTITÉS	QUANTITIES	123
L'ALPHABET	ALPHABET	126
Les COMPTINES	NURSERY RHYMES	128
Les PRIÈRES	PRAYERS	131

VOCABULARY

Family, Endearments, Colors, Days	133
Months, Seasons, Holidays, Nursery	134
Toys	135
Toys, Clothes	136
Entertainments, Human Body,	137
Human Body, Beverages, Containers, Desserts	138
Vegetables, Meat, Seafood	139
Fruits, Other Food	140
Utensils, House, Dwellings	141
Kitchen, Bathroom	142
Bedroom, Living Room, Tools	143
Car, Stores, Occupations	144
Occupations, Insects	145
Trees, Animals	146
Birds, Flowers	147
Along the Road	148

PRONUNCIATION GUIDE	149
INDEX	152
CUT, COLOR and PASTE	168

Child's name: _____

Received this book from: _____

Occasion: _____ Date: _____

First indication of child's understanding French: _____
_____

Child's first French word: _____

Child's favorite French word: _____

Favorite French books or stories: _____
_____
_____

Favorite French songs: _____
_____

Favorite French movies or videos: _____
_____
_____

Favorite French singer: _____

Favorite things to do in French: _____
_____
_____

Favorite French foods: _____
_____

ACKNOWLEDGMENTS

My thanks, as always, to my husband, Joe, for his patience, work and encouragement throughout this project.

PREFACE

This book covers the range of children's interests from infancy to teens. It is meant to cover not so much the calendar age of children, but rather their activities and interests regardless of what birthdays they have passed. This perspective is taken because children develop at different rates. It is hard to predict where they will be in their development and what their experiences will be at any particular age.

The author has researched many books in preparation for the *KIDS STUFF SERIES,* and has found this series to be unique among the vast array of books for children learning foreign languages. The *KIDS STUFF SERIES* translates phrases and sentences to answer the question, "How do you say, '........................' in French?" Because of this perspective, the user is able to speak *to* children, to carry on a conversation *with* children, and to model sentences that children can use in replying to others.

At whatever age you begin your foreign language adventure, you will find this book to be an invaluable guide for your journey.

Enjoy this book and your children. Good luck and have fun. Bonne chance!

SALUTATIONS   GREETINGS

Start your day and your conversations here. Saying the first few words of the day in French will help you build momentum to continue the rest of the day in French. Hearing French spoken will make you feel cheerful especially when it is spoken by you or to you. Bonjour!

(Dis) Allô!
(Dee) Ah-loh!

(Say) Hello!   *
(answering the telephone)

Qui est à l'appareil?
Kee eht ah lah-pah-ray?

Who's speaking?
(on the telephone)

Ici...
Ee-see...

This is...

Quelqu'un m'a-t-il téléphoné?
Kell-kuhng mah-teel tay-lay-fohng-nay?

Has anyone telephoned me?

Bonjour.
Bohng-zhoor.

Good morning. Good afternoon. Hello.

Bonsoir.
Bohng-swahr.

Good evening.

GREETINGS

Comment vas-tu?	How goes it?
Kawh-mawng vah-tew?	How are you?
Salut!	Hi!
Sahl-ewh!	
Bienvenue!	Welcome!
B'yehng-veh-newh!	
Fais comme chez toi.	Make yourself at home.
Feh kawhm shay twah.	
Très bien. Merci.	Very well. Thank you.
Treh b'yehng. Mehr-see.	
Je vais bien, merci.	I'm fine, thank you.
Zhuh vay b'yehng, mehr-see.	
Comme-ci, comme-ça!	So-so!
Kawhm see, kawhm sah!	
Est-ce que tu m'as manqué?	Did you miss me?
Ehs kuh tew mah mawng-kay?	
Embrasse-moi.	Give me a hug/ kiss. *
Awng-brass-mwah.	
Bonne nuit.	Good night.
Buhn nwee.	
Au revoir. Adieu.	Good-bye.
Oh ruh-vwahr. Ah-d'yewh.	
/Dis/ Fais/<<Au revoir.>>	/Say/ Wave/ "Good-bye."
/Dee/ Feh/<< Oh ruh-vwahr.>>	
A bientôt. A tout à l'heure.	So long. See you later.
Ah b'yehng-toh. Ah too-tah-luhr.	

GREETINGS

Je me sauve! Zhuh muh sohv!	I'm off!
Excuse-moi. Je m'excuse. Ehks-kewhz-mwah. Zhuh mehks-kewhz.	Excuse me.
Dieu te bénisse. D'yewh tuh bay-nees.	God bless you. (after a sneeze)
(A ta) santé! (Ah tah) sawng-tay!	(To your) health! (a toast)
Bon anniversaire! Bohng-ah-nee-vehr-sair!	Happy birthday! *
Joyeux Noël! Zhwah-yewh noh-well!	Merry Christmas! *
Bonne Année! Buhn-ah-nay!	Happy New Year!
Joyeuses Pâques! Zhwah-ewhz pahk!	Happy Easter!
S'il te plaît. Seel tuh pleh.	Please.
Je te demande pardon. Zhuh tuh duh-mawngd pahr-dohng.	I beg your pardon.
Merci beaucoup. Mehr-see boh-kooh.	Thank you very much.
Je t'en prie. Zhuh tawng pree.	You're welcome.
Oui. Non. Wee. Nohng.	Yes. No.

GREETINGS

Amuse-toi!   Have a good time!
Ah-mewhz-twah!

Bonne chance!   Good luck!
Buhn shahns!

Rentre bien!   Come back (return) home
Rawng-tr b'yehng!   safely!

Comment t'appelles-tu?   What is your name?
Kawh-mawng tah-pell-tew?

Je m'appelle......   My name is......
Zhuh mah-pell......

Où habites-tu?   Where do you live?
Oo ah-beet-tew?

J'habite...   I live.....
Zhah-beet....

Parles-tu français?   Do you speak French?
Pahrl-tew frawng-seh?

Je (ne) parle (pas) français.   I (don't) speak French.
Zhuh (nuh) pahrl (pah) frawng-seh.

Beaucoup de bonheur!   All the best!
Boh-kooh d'bohng-nuhr!

Je t'en prie.   It's a pleasure.
Zhuh tawng pree.

Propre comme un sou neuf. Clean as a whistle.

La SALLE de BAINS — BATHROOM

Every family member knows how much time is spent in the bathroom showering, bathing, singing, soaking, admiring. This is a good time to practice your French looking in the mirror or aloud in the shower.

As-tu besoin d'aller à la salle de bains? Ah-tew buh-zwahng dah-lay ah lah sahl d'bahng?	Do you need to go to the bathroom?
Dis-moi quand tu as besoin d'aller à la salle de bains. Dee-mwah kawng tew ah buh-zwahng dah-lay ah lah sahl d'bahng.	Tell me when you have to go to the bathroom.
Tu es gentil/ le. Tu m'as dit que tu avais besoin d'aller à la salle de bains. Tew eh zhawng-tee/ yuh. Tew mah dee kuh tew ah-vay buh-zwahng dah-lay ah lah sahl d'bahng.	You're a good/ boy/ girl/. You told me that you had to go to the bathroom.
(Ne) laisse (pas) ouverte la porte de la salle de bains. (Nuh) lehs (pah) oo-vehrt lah pohrt d'lah sahl d'bahng.	(Don't) leave the bathroom door open.

BATHROOM

Tire la chasse d'eau.
Teer lah shass doh.

Flush the toilet.

La chasse d'eau ne fonctionne pas.
Lah shass doh nuh fohng-s'yohnn pah.

The toilet does not flush.

Remets le siège de toilettes.
Ruh-meh luh s'yehzh d'twah-lett.

Put down the toilet seat.

Va te laver (les mains).
Vah tuh lah-vay (lay mahng).

Go get washed. (Go wash *
your hands.)

Ton visage est sale. Lave-le.
Tohng vee-zahzh eh sahl. Lahv-luh.

Your face is dirty. Wash it.

N'oublie pas de laver tes mains (collantes).
Noo-blee pah d' lah-vay tay mahng (koh-lawngt).

Don't forget to wash your
(sticky) hands.

As-tu lavé ton cou?
Ah-tew lah-vay tohng koo?

Did you wash your neck?

Nettoie tes ongles.
Neh-twah tay-zohng-gl.

Clean your fingernails.

Brosse tes dents.
Brawhss tay dawng.

Brush your teeth.

Sers-toi de la soie dentaire.
Sehr-twah d'lah swah dawng-tair.

Use floss.

La brosse à dents est sur le lavabo.
Lah brawhss ah dawng eh sewr luh lah-vah-boh.

Your toothbrush is on the *
sink.

Frotte fort derrière tes oreilles.
Frawhtt fawhr deh-r'yair tay-zawh-ray-yuh.

Scrub behind your ears.

Tu n'as pas lavé ta figure.
Tew nah pah lah-vay tah fee-gewhr.

You didn't wash your face.

BATHROOM

Ton visage et tes mains sont propres.
Tohng vee-zahzh ay tay mahng sohng prawh-pr.

Your face and hands are clean.

Bon! Maintenant tu as l'air propre.
Bohng! Mahng-t'nawng tew ah lair prawh-pr.

Now you look clean.

Tu as besoin de prendre un bain.
Tew ah buh-zwahng d'prawng-dr uhng bahng.

You need to take a bath.

Ouvre le robinet.
Oo-vr luh rawh-bee-nay.

Turn on the faucet.

Le robinet (d'eau chaude) ne fonctionne pas.
Luh rawh-bee-nay (doh shohd) nuh fohng-s'yohnn pah.

The (hot water) faucet doesn't work.

Ferme l'eau.
Fehrm loh.

Turn off the water.

Est-ce que je peux prendre un bain?
Ehs kuh zhuh puh prawng-dr uhng bahn?

Can I take a bath?

Prends-tu un bain?
Prawng-tew uhng bahng?

Are you taking a bath?

Je fais couler l'eau pour ton bain.
Zhuh feh koo-lay loh poor tohng bahng.

I'm running a bath for you.   *

Vois-tu l'eau qui coule?
Vwah-tew loh kee kool?

See the water run?

L'eau est trop/ chaude/ froide/ parfaite/.
Loh eh troh/ shohd/ frwahd/ pahr-feht/.

The water is too/ hot/ cold/ just right/.

Ne remplis pas trop la baignoire.
Nuh rawng-plee pah troh lah bahng-nawhr.

Don't fill the tub with too much water.

BATHROOM

Je lave/ ton cou/ ton dos/ tes genoux/ tes orteils/.
Zhuh lahv/ tohng koo/ tohng doh/ tay zhawng-noo/tay-zawhr-tay/.

I'm washing your/ neck/ back/ knees/ toes/.

Tu ne peux pas te mettre debout dans le bain.
Tew nuh puh pah tuh meh-tr day-boo dawng luh bahng.

You cannot stand up in the tub.

Rinçons-nous le dos.
Rahng-sohng-noo luh doh.

Let's rinse your back.

Utilise beaucoup de savon.
Oo-tee-leez boh-koo d' sah-vohng.

Use plenty of soap.   *

Le savon sent bon, mais il est glissant.
Luh sah-vohng sawng bohng, meh eel eh glee-sawng.

The soap smells good, but it is slippery.

Tu n'as pas besoin de tant de savon.
Tew nah pah buh-zwahng d'tawng d'sah-vohng.

You don't need so much soap.

Sèche-toi bien.
Sehsh-twah b'yehng.

Dry yourself well.

Vide la baignoire.
Veed lah bahng-nawhr.

Empty the tub.

Plis la serviette de bain.
Plee lah sehr-v'yett d' bahng.

Fold the towel.   *

Pends le gant de toilette (sur le porte-serviettes).
Pawng luh gawng d' twah-lett (sewr luh pohrt-sehr-v'yett).

Hang up the face cloth (on the towel rack).

As-tu éteint la lumière?
Ah-tew ay-tahng lah lewh-m'yair?

Did you turn out the light?

BATHROOM

Qui a laissé la lumière allumée? Kee ah leh-say lah lewh-m'yair ah-lew-may?	Who left the light on?
Aimes-tu prendre un bain? Ehm-tew prawng-dr uhng bahng?	Do you like to take a bath?
Non. Je ne l'aime pas. Nohng. Zhuh nuh lehm pah.	No. I don't like it.
La salle de bains appartient à tout le monde! Lah sahl d'bahng ah-pahr-t'yehn ah too luh mohnd!	The bathroom belongs to everybody!
Tu as besoin de te raser. Tew ah buh-zwahng d'tuh rah-zay.	You need to shave. *
Tu en mets du temps à faire la toilette! Tuh awng meh dew tawng ah fair lah twah-lett!	You're spending a lot of time getting washed!
Lave-toi les cheveux plus tard! Lahv-twah lay shuh-vuh plewh tahr!	Wash your hair later!
Avons-nous du shampooing? Ah-vohng-noo dewh shawng-poo-ing?	Have we any shampoo?
Tu as l'air bien. Tew ah lair b'yehng.	You look good.
(or)	
Tu as bonne mine. Tew ah buhn meen.	You look good.

Il faut travailler pour vivre. One must work for a living.

| S'HABILLER | GETTING DRESSED |

Is it to be the cowboy outfit or the space suit this morning? When you are in a hurry these are not options. Perhaps, instead, when your little girl dresses her dolls or your little guy is playing with his action figures, you and they can try some of these phrases.

Debout! Il est temps de se réveiller! Day-boo! Eel eh tawng d'suh ray-vay-yay!	Get up! It's time to wake up!
Le réveil a sonné! Luh ray-veh-ah soh-nay!	The alarm clock has rung!
Je change ta couche. Zhuh shawngzh tah koosh.	I'm changing your diaper.
Mets ta main dans la manche. Meh tah mahng dawng lah mawngsh.	Put your hand through the sleeve.
Mets ton pied dans le pantalon. Meh tohng p'yay dawng luh pawng-tah-lohng.	Put your foot in the pants.
Je mets ton pied droit dans le soulier droit. Zhuh meh tohng p'yay drwah dawng luh soo-lyay drwah.	I am putting your right foot into your right shoe.

GETTING DRESSED

Tu as le pied dans le mauvais soulier.
Tew ah luh p'yay dawng luh moh-veh soo-lyay.

You have your foot in the wrong shoe. *

Veux-tu porter la blouse bleue ou la rouge?
Vuh-tew pawhr-tay lah blooz blewh oo lah roozh?

Do you want to wear the blue blouse or the red one?

Boutonne ta chemise.
Boo-tawhn tah shuh-meez.

Button your shirt. *

Où est ton chapeau?
Oo eh tohng shah-poh?

Where is your hat?

L'as-tu enfin trouvé?
Lah-tew awng-fahng troo-vay?

Did you finally find it?

Ferme la fermeture éclair de ta veste.
Fehrm lah fehr-meh-tewhr ay-klair d'tah vehst.

Close the zipper of your jacket. *

Cherche tes gants.
Shehrsh tay gawng.

Look for your gloves. *

Faisons briller tes souliers.
Feh-zohng bree-yay tay soo-lyay.

Let's polish your shoes.

Il faut que tu t'habilles.
Eel foh kuh tew tah-bee-yuh.

You must dress yourself.

Papa est parti travailler.
Pah-pah eh pahr-tee trah-vigh-yay.

Daddy has gone to work.

Habille-toi.
Ah-bee-twah.

Get dressed.

Il faut nous habiller.
Eel foh noo-zah-bee-yay.

We must get dressed.

Je m'habille tout/e seul/e. (m/f)
Zhuh mah-bee-yuh too/ t suhl.

I'm getting dressed all by myself.

GETTING DRESSED

Ne ronge pas tes ongles.
Nuh rohnzh pah tay-zohng-gl.

Don't bite your nails.

Enfile tes sous-vêtements et ton pantalon.
Awng-feel tay soo-veht-mawng ay tohng pawng-tah-lohng.

Put on your underwear and pants. *

Porte ton nouveau manteau.
Pawhrt tohng noo-voh mawng-toh.

Wear your new coat. *

Va chercher tes nouveaux souliers.
Vah shehr-shay tay noo-voh soo-lyay.

Go get your new shoes.

Laisse-moi t'aider à attacher tes lacets.
Lehs-mwah teh-day ah ah-tash-ay tay lah-seh.

Let me help you tie your shoe laces. *

Il y a un noeud à ton lacet.
Eel ee ah uhng nuh ah tohng lah-seh.

There is a knot in your shoe lace.

Peigne-toi.
Pehn-twah.

Comb your hair.

Brosse-toi les cheveux.
Brawhss-twah lay shuh-vuh.

Brush your hair.

La brosse, le peigne et la lime à ongles sont sur la commode.
Lah brawhss, luh pehn-yuh ay lah leem ah ohng-gl sohng sewr lah koh-mohd.

The brush, comb and nail file are on the dresser. *

Tu ne te sers pas de rouge à lèvres.
Tew nuh tuh sehr pah d'roozh ah leh-vreh.

You may not use lipstick.

Comme tu es beau/ belle! (m/f)
Kawhm tew eh boh/ bell!

How nice you look!

Comme tu as l'air joyeux!
Kawhm tew ah lair zhwah-yewh!

How happy you look!

premier arrivé, premier servi. **First come, first served.**

L'HEURE du REPAS   MEALTIME

Mark the "Beverages," "Desserts," and "Meats," pages of this book in order to expand your foods vocabulary. You might even want to pretend that you and your children are one of the birds from the "Birds" page, and select the "Insects" you might find appetizing. (Something to do *after* mealtime!) Bon appétit!

Veux-tu prendre le petit déjeuner?   Do you want breakfast?
Vuh-tew prawng-dr 1uh p'tee day-zhuh-nay?

Viens prendre tes céréales.   Come and get your cereal.
V'yehng prawng-dr tay say-ray-ahl.

Quand déjeunons-nous?   When are we having lunch?
Kawng day-zhuhng-nohng-noo?

Qu'est-ce que tu voudrais manger?   What would you like to eat?
Kehs kuh tew voo-dray mawng-zhay?

Qu'est-ce qu'il y a à /manger/ boire/?   What is there to /eat/ drink/?
Kehs keel-ee-ah ah /mawng-zhay/ bwahr/?

MEALTIME

Tu n'as rien mangé. Tew nah r'yehng mawng-zhay.	You have not eaten anything.
Quand est-ce qu'on mange? Kawng ehs kohng mawngzh?	When are we eating?
Maman nous appelle pour dîner. Mah-mawng nouz-ah-pell poor dee-nay.	Mom is calling us for dinner.
Le dîner est prêt. A table. Luh dee-nay eh preh. Ah tah-bl.	Diner is ready. Come to the table.
Prends ta place. Prawng tah plahs.	Take your seat.
Assieds-toi près de la table. Ah-syay-twah preh d' lah tah-bl.	Sit close to the table.
Ne mets pas les coudes sur la table. Nuh meh pah lay kood sewr lah tah-bl.	Don't put your elbows on the table.
Voudrais-tu un bon casse-croûte? Voo-dray-tew uhng bohng kass-kroot?	Would you like a nice snack?
Veux-tu du lard ou des pommes de terre? Vuh-tew dew lahr oo day pawhm d'tair?	Do you want bacon or potatoes?
Sers-toi. Sehr-twah.	Help yourself.
Fais-toi un sandwich. Feh-twah uhng sawngd-weech.	Fix yourself a sandwich. *
Fais réchauffer la pizza dans le four à micro-onde. Feh ray-shoh-fay lah peed-zah dawng luh foor ah mee-kroh-ohnd.	Warm up the pizza in the microwave oven.
Puis-je avoir encore des carottes? Pweezh ah-vwahr awng-kawhr day kah-rawht?	May I have more carrots?

_____MEALTIME

Tu en veux encore? Tew awng vuh awng-kawhr?	Do you want more?
Tu en voudrais encore? Tew awng voo-dray zawng-kawhr?	Would you want more? (More polite form)
En reste-t-il pour moi? Awng rest-teel poor mwah?	Is there any more (of it/ of them) left for me?
Je prendrai un peu plus de céréales. Zhuh prawng-dray uhng puh plewh d'say-ray-ahl.	I'll take a little more cereal.
Je n'en veux plus. Zhuh nawng vuh plewh.	I don't want /any more/ it/.
Veux-tu passer le sel? Vuh-tew pah-say luh sehl?	Will you pass the salt? *
Sers-toi de/ ta fourchette/ ton couteau/ ta cuiller/. Sehr-twah duh/ tah fohr-shett/ tohng koo-toh/ tah kwee-yehr/.	Use your /fork/ knife/ spoon/.
N'écrase pas ta banane dans la main. Nay-krahs pah tah bah-nahng dawng lah mahng.	Don't squeeze the banana in your hand. *
Mange la pomme mûre, mais fais attention aux pépins. Mawngzh lah pawhm mewhr, meh feh-zah-tawng-s'yohng oh pay-pahng.	Eat the ripe apple, but be careful of the pits. *
Laisse-moi couper ta viande. Lehs-mwah koo-pay tah vee-awngd.	Let me cut your meat.
Quelqu'un veut des hot dogs? Kell-kuhng vuh day hawht dawhg?	Anyone want hot dogs? *
Ne bois pas le lait si vite. Nuh bwah pah luh lay see veet.	Don't drink your milk so fast.

27

MEALTIME

Mâche bien la nourriture.
Mahsh b'yehng lah noor-ee-tewhr.

Chew your food well.

Mange /ta viande/ tes épinards/.
Mawngzh /tah vee-awngd/ tay-zay-peen-ahr/.

Eat /your meat/ your spinach/.

Mange un tout petit peu.
Mawngzh uhng too p'tee puh.

Eat just a little.

Mets les miettes dans l'assiette.
Meh lay mee-ett dawng lah-s'yett.

Put the crumbs on the plate.

La nourriture sent /bon/ mauvais/.
Lah noor-ee-tewhr sawng /bohng/ moh-veh/.

The food smells /good/ bad/.

C'est aigre.
Set-ay-gr.

It is sour.

Le café est amer.
Luh kah-fay eh-tah-mehr.

The coffee is bitter.

Le dessert est sucré.
Luh duh-sehr eh soo-kray.

The dessert is sweet.   *

La sauce est fade.
Lah sohs eh fahd.

The sauce is flat.

Le poisson est trop salé.
Luh pwah-sohng eh troh sah-lay.

The fish is too salty.   *

Le biftek est saignant.
Luh beef-tehk eh seh-nyawng.

The steak is rare.

Aimes-tu le fromage?
Ehm-tew luh frawh-mahzh?

Do you like cheese?

Voudrais-tu une petite goutte de thé?
Voo-dray-tew ewn p'teet goot d' tay?

Would you like a sip of tea?

MEALTIME

Puis-je faire goûter la soupe?
Pweezh fair goo-tay lah soop?

Can I taste your soup?

Prends-en encore.
Prawng-zawng awng-kawhr.

Take some more.

J'aime les pois.
Zhem lay pwah.

I like peas.

Tu peux manger tout seul. Essaie.
Tew puh mawng-zhay too suhl.
Eh-say.

You can feed yourself.
Try it.

Tu as de la nourriture sur tout ton visage.
Tew ah d'lah noor-ee-tewhr sewr too tohng vee-zahzh.

You have food all over your face.

Ne parle pas la bouche pleine.
Nuh pahrl pah lah boosh plehn.

Don't speak with your mouth full.

Verse le lait dans le verre.
Vehrs luh lay dawng luh vair.

Pour the milk in the glass.

Coupe soigneusement le pain.
Koop swahng-yuhz-mawng luh pahng.

Cut the bread carefully. *

Ne remplis pas le verre.
Nuh rawng-plee pah luh vair.

Don't fill the glass.

Ne renverse pas l'eau.
Nuh rawng-vehrs pah loh.

Don't spill the water.

Tu as renversé le lait.
Tew ah rawng-vehr-say luh lay.

You spilt the milk.

Pourquoi faut-il manger tellement?
Poor-kwah foh-teel mawng-zhay tell-mawng?

Why must you eat so much?

Finis ton/ repas/ jus/.
Fee-nee tohng/ ruh-pah/ zhew/.

Finish your/ meal/ juice/.

29

MEALTIME

As-tu fini de manger?
Ah-tew fee-nee d'mawng-zhay?

Have you finished eating?

Finis de boire ton lait avant de quitter la table.
Fee-nee d' bwahr tohng lay ah-vawng duh kee-tay lah tah-bl.

Drink up your milk before leaving the table.

Tout fini!
Too fee-nee!

All gone!

Tu as mangé toute ton assiette.
Tew ah mawng-zhay toot tawng-nah-s'yett.

You've eaten everything on your plate.

Bon appétit.
Boh-nah-peh-tee.

Enjoy your meal.

Oh! Que c'est délicieux!
Oh! Kuh seh day-lee-syuh!

Oh! How delicious!

Quel bon /goûter/ petit déjeuner/ déjeuner/ dîner/!
Kell bohng/ goo-tay/ p'tee day-zhuh-nay/ day-zhuh-nay/ dee-nay/!

What a good /snack/ breakfast/ lunch/ dinner/!

C'est en forgeant qu'on devient forgeron. Practice makes perfect.

CONVERSATIONS   CONVERSATIONS

These are the pages you use to enlist, explain, persuade, coax, and insist with your child. When all else fails, there is always, <<Parce que je le dis.>> ("Because I say so!") — appropriate justification in any language.

Qu'est-ce que tu entends?   What do you hear?
Kehs kuh tew awng-tawng?

Quel bruit!   What a noise!
Kell brwee!

Est-ce que je t'ai fait peur?   Did I frighten you?
Ehs kuh zhuh tay feh puhr?

Que dis-tu? (or) Qu'est-ce que tu dis? What are you saying?
Kuh dee tew? (or) Kehs kuh tew dee?

Qu'est-ce que tu as dit?   What did you say?
Kehs kuh tew ah dee?

J'écoute. (Je t'écoute.)   I'm listening (to you).
Zhay-koot. (Zhuh tay-koot.)

CONVERSATIONS

Que tu chantes bien! How well you sing! *
Kuh tew shahnt b'yehng!

Que tu es bavard/e! (m/f) How talkative you are!
Kuh tew eh bah-vahr/d!

Tiens-toi droit. Sit up straight.
T'yehng-twah drwah.

Assieds-toi sur mes genoux. Come sit on my lap.
Ah-s'yay-twah sewr may zhawng-noo.

Lève la tête. Raise your head.
Lehv lah teht.

Comme tu es fort/e! (m/f) How strong you are!
Kawhm tew eh fawhr/t!

Tiens-le/-la. (m/f) Tiens bon! Hold it. Hold on!
T'yehng-luh/-lah. T'yehng bohng!

Tiens le hochet. Hold the rattle. *
T'yehng luh oh-sheh.

Lâche prise! Let go!
Lahsh preez!

Qu'est-ce que tu regardes? What are you looking
Kehs kuh tew ruh-gahrd? at?

A quoi penses-tu? What are you thinking
Ah kwah pawngs-tew? about?

Je vois que tu rêves. I see that you're dream-
Zhuh vwah que tew rehv. ing.

Tourne tes bras et tes jambes! Move your arms and legs!
Toorn tay brah ay tay zhahmb!

CONVERSATIONS

Qui suis-je?
Kee sweezh?

Who am I?

Qui est-ce?
Kee ehs?

Who is it?

Je te connais.
Zhuh tuh kawng-neh.

I know you.

C'est ton frère, ta soeur.
Seh tohng frair, tah suhr.

It's your brother,
your sister.

/Il/ Elle/ est grand/e. (m/f)
/Eel/ Ell/ eh grawnh/d.

/He/ She/ is tall.

/Il/ Elle/ est petit/e. (m/f)
/Eel/ Ell/ eh p'tee/ t.

/He/ She/ is small.

Tes yeux sont pareils à ceux de papa.
Tayz-yuh sohng pah-ray ah suh d'pah-pah.

You have eyes like Daddy's.

Souris! Fais-moi un grand sourire!
Soo-ree! Feh-mwah uhng grawng soo-reer!

Smile! Show me a big smile!

Voici ton nez, ta bouche, ton oreille.
Vwah-see tohng nay, tah boosh, tohng-nawh-ray-yuh.

Here is your nose, your mouth, your ear.

Je veux prendre ta photo.
Zhuh vuh prawng-dr tah foh-toh.

I want to take your picture.   *

Quelle longue histoire!
Kell lohng-ee-stwahr!

What a long story!

Laisse-moi frotter ton ventre.
Lehs-mwah frawh-tay tohng vawng-tr.

Let me rub your tummy.

Où vas-tu?
Oo vah-tew?

Where are you going?

CONVERSATIONS

Vite! Pas si vite! Veet! Pah see veet!	Quick! Not so quick!
Roule-toi. Rool-twah.	Roll over.
Vois-tu...? Vwah-tew...?	Do you see?
Peux-tu tenir la souris? Puh-tew tuh-neer lah soo-ree?	Can you hold the mouse? *
Qu'est-ce que tu as dans / la bouche/ la main/? Kehs kuh tew ah dawng / lah boosh/ lah mahng/?	What do you have in your / mouth/ hand/?
Ne mets pas ça dans la bouche. Nuh meh pah sah dawng lah boosh.	Don't put that in your mouth.
Pas d'éclaboussures! Suffit! Pah day-klah-boo-sewhr! Soo-fee!	No splashing! Stop it!
Comme tu tapes du pied! Kawhm tew tapp dew p'yay!	How you kick!
Tu me fais mouiller! Tew muh feh moo-yay!	You're getting me wet!
Qui vois-tu dans la glace? Kee vwah-tew dawng lah glahs?	Whom do you see in the mirror? *
Qui t'aime? Kee tehm?	Who loves you?
Veux-tu jouer à la balle? Vuh-tew zhoo-ay ah lah bahl?	Do you want to play ball? *
/Le/ La/ voici.(m/f) Vois toi-même. /Luh/ Lah/ vwah-see. Vwah twah-mehm.	Here it is. See for yourself.

34

_____CONVERSATIONS

Nous allons rendre visite à grand-mère. Nooz-ah-lohng rawng-dr vee-zeet ah grawng-mair.	We're going to visit grandma.
Prépare-toi (à partir). Pray-pahr-twah (ah pahr-teer).	Get ready (to go).
Viens vers maman. V'yehng vehr mah-mawng.	Come to mommy.
Voyons comment tu marches. Vwah-yohng kawh-mawng tew mahrsh.	Let's see how you walk.
Regarde ces dents! Ruh-gahrd say dawng!	Look at those teeth! *
Les dents te font mal? Lay dawng tuh fohng mahl?	Do your teeth hurt?
Pas si fort! Pah see fohr!	Not so loud!
Bats le tambour. Sonne la cloche. Bah luh tahng-boor. Sawhng lah klahsh.	Bang the drum. Ring the bell. *
Claque les mains. Klahk lay mahng.	Clap your hands.
Voici un bébé comme toi. Vwah-see uhng bay-bay kawhm twah.	Here is a baby like you.
Où sont les pieds, les yeux du bébé? Oo sohng lay p'yay, layz-yuh dew bay-bay?	Where are the feet, the eyes of the baby?
Il nous faut faire une visite chez le médecin. Eel noo foh fair ewn vee-zeet shay luh mayd-sahng.	We have to go to the doctor's.
C'est le moment du bilan de santé. Seh luh moh-mawng dew bee-lawng d'sawhn-tay.	It's time for a check-up.

35

CONVERSATIONS
_____

Maman est ici.   Mommy is here.
Mah-mahng eht-ee-see.

Tu n'aimes pas...?   Don't you like...?
Tew nehm pah...?

Tu ne veux pas...?   Don't you want...?
Tew nuh vuh pah...?

Allons nous promener.   Let's go for a little walk.
Ah-lohng noo prawh-m'nay.

Arrête de:/ Défense de: Stop:/ No:
Ah-reht duh: / Day-fawngs duh:

    pousser du pied,   kicking,
    poo-say dew p'yay,

    frapper,   hitting,
    frah-pay,

    mordre,   biting,
    mawhr-dr,

    pleurer.   crying.
    pluh-ray.

Arrête-toi!   Stop! Cut it out!
Ah-reht-twah!

Ça me fait mal.   That hurts me.
Sah muh feh mahl.

Défense d'entrer!   No admittance!
Day-fawngs dawng-tray!

Donne-moi la main.   Give me your hand.
Dawhn-mwah lah mahng.

_____CONVERSATIONS

Ne me donne pas...   Don't give me . . .
Nuh muh dawhn pah...

Donne-le/-moi/ à papa/.   Give it /to me/ to Daddy/.
Dawhn-luh/-mwah/ ah pah-pah/

Lâche-le.   Let go of it.
Lahsh-luh.

Tends la main pour prendre le cube.   Reach for the block.   *
Tawng lah mahng poor prawng-dr luh kewb.

Ne fais pas tant de bruit.   Don't make so much noise.
Nuh feh pah tawng d'brwee.

Qu'est-ce qui se passe?   What's going on?
Kehs kee suh pahs?

Silence, s'il te plait.   Quiet, please.
See-lawngs, seel tuh pleh.

Tais-toi. Chut!   Be quiet. Sh-h-h-h!
Teh-twah. Shewt!

Ne me demande pas encore.   Don't ask me again.
Nuh muh duh-mawngd pah-zawng-kawhr.

Demande si tu peux...+ inf   Ask if you may...+ inf
Duh-mawngd see tew puh...+ inf

Je suis occupé/e maintenant. (m/f)   I'm busy now.
Zhuh swee-zock-ew-pay mahng-t'nawng.

Je suis pressé/e. (m/f)   I'm in a hurry.
Zhuh swee preh-say.

Il faut que je parte.   I must go.
Eel foh kuh zhuh pahrt.

CONVERSATIONS

Je reviendrai plus tard.
Zhuh ruh-v'yehng-dray plewh tahr.

I'll come back later.

Attends! (un instant)
Ah-tawng! (-zuhng-nahng-stawng)

Wait! (a moment)

Attends-moi à / l'extérieur/ l'intérieur/.
Ah-tawng-mwah ah /lehks-tehr-y'uhr/ lahng-tehr-y'uhr/.

Wait for me/ outside/ inside/.

On s'en va!
Ohng sawng vah!

Let's go out!

Il faut rester à la maison.
Eel foh reh-stay ah lah meh-zohng.

You have to stay inside (the house).

Je vais venir dans un instant.
Zhuh veh vuh-neer dawng-zuhng-nahng-stawng.

I'm coming in a moment.

Attends jusqu'à ce que je revienne.
Ah-tawng zhews-kah s'kuh zhuh ruh-v'yehnne.

Wait until I come back.

Je veux te parler.
Zhuh vuh tuh pahr-lay.

I want to talk to you.

Nous parlerons de cela plus tard.
Noo pahrl-rohng d'suh-lah plewh tahr.

We'll talk about that later.

Ne bouge pas.
Nuh boozh pah.

Don't move.

Fais demi-tour.
Feh deh-mee-toor.

Turn around.

Ne me quitte pas. Va-t'en.
Nuh muh keet pah. Vah-tawng.

Don't go away. Go away.

Arrête de faire ça.
Ah-reht d' fair sah.

Stop doing that.

Continue jusqu'à ce que je te dise d'arrêter. Kawng-tee-newh zhews-kah s'kuh zhuh tuh deez dah-reh-tay.	Go until I tell you to stop.
Viens ici. V'yehng ee-see.	Come away from there. (Come here.)
Viens voir. V'yehng vwahr.	Come see.
Fais ce que je te dis! Feh s'kuh zhuh tuh dee!	Do what I tell you!
Tu (n') es (pas) censé...+ inf. Tew (n) eh (pah) sawng-say...	You're (not) supposed to... + inf.
Tu le feras, d'une façon ou d'une autre. Tew luh feh-rah, dewn fah-sohng oo dewn oh-truh.	You will do it, one way or the other.
Fais ce que tu veux. Feh s'kuh tew vuh.	Do what you like.
Ne me dérange pas. Nuh muh day-rawngzh pah.	Don't give me trouble.
Ne me désobéis pas. Nuh muh day-zoh-bay-ee pah.	Don't disobey me.
Ne vous battez pas; chacun son tour. Nuh voo bah-tay pah; shah-kuhng sohng toor.	Don't fight; take turns. (More than one)
Ne vous disputez pas. Nuh voo dee-spewh-tay pah.	Don't quarrel. (More than one child.)
Laisse-le tranquille. Lehs-luh trawng-keel.	Leave him alone.

CONVERSATIONS

Laisse la chatte (f) tranquille. Ne la taquine pas.	Leave the cat alone.	*
Lehs lah shaht (f) trawng-keel. Nuh lah tah-keen pah.	Don't tease her.	

Caresse le chien (doucement). Pet the dog (gently). *
Kah-rehss luh sh'ehng (doos-mawng).

Laisse-ça. Leave that alone.
Lehs-sah.

Ne le casse pas. Don't break it.
Nuh luh kass pah.

Ne touche pas (ça). C'est sale. Don't touch (that).
Nuh toosh pah (sah). Seh sahl. It's dirty.

Ne ramasse pas cela. Don't pick that up.
Nuh rah-mass pah suh-lah.

Ne touche pas à mes outils! Don't touch my tools!
Nuh toosh pah ah mayz-oo-tee!

A bas les mains! Hands off!
Ah bah lay mahng!

Ouvre la porte. Ne ferme pas la porte à clé. Open the door. *
Oo-vr lah pawhrt. Nuh fehrm pah lah pawhrt Don't lock the door.
ah klay.

N'ouvre pas la fenêtre. Don't open the window.
Noo-vr pah lah fuh-neh-tr.

Ne te penche pas par la fenêtre. Don't lean out of the
Nuh tuh pawngsh pah pahr lah fuh-neh-tr. window.

Ferme le frigo. Close the refrigerator.
Fehrm luh free-goh.

Ne ferme pas la boîte. Don't close the box.
Nuh fehrm pah lah bwaht.

40

CONVERSATIONS

Mets la boîte là-bas.
Meh lah bwaht lah-bah.

Put the box over there.   *

Une place pour chaque chose et chaque
chose à sa place.
Ewn plahs poor shahk shohz ay shahk
shohz ah sah plahs.

A place for everything and
everything in its place.

Saute! Ne saute pas!
Soht! Nuh soht pah!

Jump! Don't jump!

Ralentis!
Rah-lawng-tee!

Slow down!

Ne cours pas. Marche!
Nuh koor pah. Mahrsh!

Don't run. Walk!

Va te promener.
Vah tuh prawh-m'nay.

Go for a walk.

Regarde où tu marches.
Ruh-gahrd oo tew mahrsh.

Look where you are
walking.

Ne te dépêche pas. Tu vas tomber.
Nuh tuh day-pehsh pah. Tew vah tawng-bay.

Don't hurry.
You are going to fall.

Prends garde de ne pas tomber.
Prawng gahrd d'nuh pah tawng-bay.

Take care not to fall.

Prends ton temps.
Prawng tohng tawng.

Take your time.

Dépêche-toi!
Day-pehsh-twah!

Hurry!

Nous devons nous dépêcher!
Noo duh-vohng noo day-pehsh-ay!

We must hurry!

Nous devons partir.
Noo duh-vohng pahr-teer.

We must go.

CONVERSATIONS

Mange dans la cuisine pour ne pas tâcher le tapis.
Mawngzh dawng lah kwee-zeen poor nuh pah tah-shay luh tah-pee.

Eat in the kitchen so that you don't stain the rug.

N'oublie pas d'essuyer les pieds.
Noo-blee pah deh-swee-yay lay p'yay.

Don't forget to wipe your feet.

Remets le soulier à sa place.
Ruh-meh luh soo-lyay ah sah plahs.

Put the shoe back in its place.   *

La chaussure va sur le plancher.
Lah shoh-sewhr vah sewr luh plawng-shay.

The shoe belongs on the floor.

Recule!
Ruh-kewl!

Stand back!

Ne touche pas le fourneau.
Nuh toosh pah luh foor-noh.

Don't touch the stove.

Tu vas te brûler.
Tew vah tuh brewl-yay.

You are going to burn yourself.

Est-ce que tu t'es brûlé/e? (m/f)
Ehs kuh tew teh brewl-yay?

Did you burn yourself?

Ne joue pas avec les allumettes.
Nuh zhoo pah ah-vek lay-zah-lewh-mett.

Don't play with matches.   *

Ne va pas près des escaliers.
Nuh vah pah preh day-zehs-kah-lyay.

Don't go near the stairs.

Monte les escaliers (jusqu'en haut).
Mohngt lay-zehs-kah-lyay (zhews-kawng-oh).

Climb the stairs (right to the top).   *

Descends les escaliers doucement.
Day-sawng lay-zehs-kah-lyay doos-mawng.

Come down the stairs carefully.

Ne tourne pas à mi-chemin.
Nuh toorn pah ah mee-shuh-mahng.

Don't turn around half-way.

_____CONVERSATIONS

Attention à la marche.
Ah-tawng-s'yohng ah lah mahrsh.

Ne traverse pas la rue (sans moi).
Nuh trah-vehrs pah lah rewh (sawng mwah).

Regarde des deux côtés avant de traverser.
Ruh-gahrd day duh koh-tay ah-vawng d'
trah-vehr-say.

Attends le feu vert.
Ah-tawng luh fuh vehr.

A partir de maintenant, prends garde!
Ah pahr-teer d' mahng-t'nawng, prawng gahrd!

Fais attention!
Feh-zah-tawng-s'yohng!

Prends-en soin.
Prawng-zawng swahng.

Tiens-le /par la poignée/ à deux mains/.
T'yehng-luh /pahr lah pwah-nyay/
ah duh mahng/.

Fais attention à ce que tu fais.
Feh-zah-tawng-s'yohng ah s'kuh tew feh.

Fais attention à ton travail.
Feh-zah-tawng-s'yohng ah tohng trah-vigh.

Ne le laisse pas tomber par terre.
Nuh luh lehs pah tawng-bay pahr tair.

Ne coupe pas ton doigt; le couteau est très coupant.
Nuh koop pah tohng dwah; luh koo-toh
eh treh koo-pawng.

Watch the step.

Don't cross the street (without me).

Look both ways before crossing.

Wait for the green light.   *

From now on, be careful!

Be careful!

Take care of it.

Hold it /by the handle/with two hands/.

Pay attention to what you are doing.

Pay attention to your work.

Don't drop it on the ground.

Don't cut your finger; the knife is sharp.   *

CONVERSATIONS

Ne saisis pas ça. Nuh seh-zee pah sah.	Don't grab that.
... parce que je le dis. ... pahrs kuh zhuh luh dee.	... because I say so.
... parce que c'est comme ça. ... pahrs kuh seh kawhm sah.	... because that's the way it is.
S'il te plaît, pourrais-tu... (m'apporter le balai à laver)? Seel tuh pleh, poor-ay-tew ... (mah-pawhr-tay luh bah-lay ah lah-vay)?	Could you please... (bring me the mop)?
Penses-tu que... (tu pourrais m'aider à préparer le déjeuner)? Pawngs-tew kuh ... (tew poor-ay meh-day ah pray-pah-ray luh day-zhuh-nay)?	Do you think that... (you could help me prepare lunch)?
Penses-tu que tu peux... (porter l'assiette)? Pawngs-tew kuh tew puh... (pawhr-tay lah-s'yett)?	Do you think that you can... (carry the dish)?
/Porte/ Prends/ ça. /Pohrt/ Prawng/ sah.	/Carry / Take/ this/ that/.
Emporte-le! Ahng-pawhrt-luh!	Take it away!
Qu'as-tu dans la main? Kah-tew dawng lah mahng?	What do you have in your hand?
Puis-je demander... (pourquoi tu as jeté cette pierre)? Pweezh duh-mawng-day... (poor-kwah tew ah zheh-tay sett p'yair)?	May I ask you...(why you threw that rock)?
Que pouvons-nous faire? Kuh poo-vohng-noo fair?	What can we do?

CONVERSATIONS

Essayons ensemble. Eh-say-ohng-zawng-sawng-bl.	Let's try together.
Fais monter ton frère. Feh mohng-tay tohng frair.	Have your brother come upstairs.
Où es-tu? En haut ou en bas? Oo eh-tew? Awng-oh oo awng bah?	Where are you? Upstairs or downstairs?
Dis-lui de venir. Dee-l'wee duh vuh-neer.	Tell him to come.
Fais entrer ta soeur. Feh-zawng-tray tah suhr.	Have your sister come in.
Je veux/ le/ la/ voir. Zhuh vuh /luh/ lah/ vwahr.	I want to see /him/ her/.
Tu as sali ta chemise. Tew ah sah-lee tah shuh-meez.	You have dirtied your shirt. *
Va dans ta chambre, et mets une autre chemise. Vah dawng tah shawng-br, ay meh-zewn oh-tr shuh-meez.	Go into your room, and put on another shirt.
Vide tes poches. Veed tay pohsh.	Empty your pockets.
Montre-moi le chemin de ta chambre. Mawng-tr-mwah luh shuh-mahng duh tah shawng-br.	Show me the way to your room.
Qu'est-ce que tu fais? Keh kuh tew feh?	What are you doing/ making?
Laisse/- le/- la/ faire ça. Lehs/-luh/- lah/ fair sah.	Let / him/ her/ do it.

CONVERSATIONS

Sois gentil/ le/ avec/ lui/ elle/. (m/f) Swah zhohng-tee/ tee-yuh/ ah-vek / l'wee/ ell/.	Be kind (m/f) with /him/ her/.
Assieds-toi. Reste assis/e. (m/f) Ah-syay-twah. Rest ah-see/z.	Sit down. Remain seated.
Assieds-toi sur ta chaise. Ah-syay-twah sewr tah shehz.	Sit in your chair.
Ne grimpe pas sur ça. Nuh grahnp pah sewr sah.	Don't climb up on that.
Descends de cette chaise! Day-sawng d'sett shehz!	Get down from that chair! *
Mets-toi debout. Reste debout. Meh-twah day-boo. Rest day-boo.	Stand up. Remain standing.
Couche-toi. Koosh-twah.	Lie down.
Je suis en train de m'allonger. Zhuh sweez-awng trahng d'mah-lohng-zhay.	I am (in the process of) lying down.
Berce le bébé gentiment. Behrs luh bay-bay zhawng-tee-mawng.	Rock the baby gently.
Va voir si le bébé dort. Vah vwahr see luh bay-bay dohr.	Go see if the baby's sleeping.
Dis-moi ce qui est arrivé. Dee-mwah s'kee eh-tah-ree-vay.	Tell me what happened.
Sais-tu comment c'est arrivé? Say-tew kawh-mawng seh-tah-ree-vay?	Do you know how it happened?
Est-ce toi qui l'a fait? Ehs twah kee lah feh?	Was it you who did it?

CONVERSATIONS

L'as-tu fait exprès?
Lah-tew feh ehks-preh?

Did you do it on purpose?

Je ne l'ai pas fait exprès.
Zhuh nuh lay pah feh ehks-preh.

I didn't do it on purpose.

Fais attention à ton langage.
Feh-zah-tawng-s'yohng ah tohng lawng-gahzh.

Watch your language.

Je te parle.
Zhuh tuh pahrl.

I'm speaking to you.

Je veux que tu me dises la vérité.
Zhuh vuh kuh tew muh deez lah vay-ree-tay.

I want you to tell me the truth.

Il vaut mieux dire la vérité.
Eel voh m'yewh deer lah veh-ree-tay.

It's better to tell the truth.

Parle plus /lentement/ clairement/.
Pahrl plewh/ lawngt-mawng/ klair-mawng/.

Speak more /slowly/ clearly/.

Ecoute soigneusement.
Ay-koot swahng-yuhz-mawng.

Listen carefully.

Tu ne te tiens pas bien aujourd'hui.
Tew nuh tuh t'yehng pah b'yehng oh-zhoor-dwee.

You are not behaving well today.

Tu ne t'es pas bien tenu.
Tew nuh teh pah b'yehng tuh-newh.

You did not behave well.

Promets-moi de bien te tenir.
Proh-meh-mwah d' b'yehng tuh tuh-neer.

Promise me to behave.

Tiens-toi bien.
T'yehng-twah b'yehng.

Behave yourself.

Ne sois pas de mauvaise humeur.
Nuh swah pah d'mau-vehz ewh-muhr.

Don't be cross.

CONVERSATIONS

Ne te mets pas en colère contre moi.
Nuh tuh meh pah awng koh-lehr kawng-tr mwah.

Don't get angry with me.

Comprends-tu ce que je dis?
Kohng-prawng-tew s'kuh zhuh dee?

Do you understand what I'm saying?

Sois sage.
Swah sahzh.

Be good.

Ne sois pas vilain/e. (m/f)
Nuh swah pah vee-lahng/nn.

Don't be naughty.

Comme tu es têtu/e! (m/f)
Kawhm tew eh teh-tewh!

Are you stubborn!

Comme tu es gâté/e!
Kawhm tew es gah-tay!

Are you spoiled!

Ne pleure pas. Calme-toi.
Nuh pluhr pah. Kahlm-twah.

Don't cry. Calm down.

Sèche tes larmes et joue avec moi.
Sehsh tay lahrm ay zhoo ah-vek mwah.

Dry your tears and play with me.

Ne sois pas nerveux/use. (m/f)
Nuh swah pah nehr-vuh/ vuhz.

Don't be nervous.

N'aie pas peur. Tout s'arrangera.
Nay pah puhr. Too sah-rawngzh-rah.

Don't be afraid. Everything will be all right.

Montre-moi où ça te fait mal.
Mawng-tr-mwah oo sah tuh feh mahl.

Show me where it hurts.

Tu t'es fait une bosse au nez.
Tew teh feh-tewn bawhs oh nay.

You bumped your nose.

Frotte-le avec la main.
Frawhtt-luh ah-vek lah mahng.

Rub it with your hand.

CONVERSATIONS

Ne mets pas ce caillou dans ta bouche;
plutôt, touche-le.
Nuh meh pah suh kigh-yoo dawng tah boosh;
plewh-toh, toosh-luh.

Don't put that pebble in your mouth; rather, feel it.

Ne fais pas de grimaces.
Nuh feh pah d'gree-mahs.

Don't make faces.

Cela te fera du bien.
Suh-lah tuh feh-rah dew b'yehng.

It will do you good.

Mouche-toi.
Moosh-twah.

Blow your nose.

Respire par le nez.
Reh-speer pahr luh nay.

Breathe through your nose.

Ne me dis pas que tu...
Nuh muh dee pah kuh tew...

Don't tell me that you...

Dis-moi tout ce que tu sais.
Dee-mwah too s'kuh tew say.

Tell me all you know.

Sais-tu de quoi tu parles?
Say-tew d'kwah tew pahrl?

Do you know what you're talking about?

Qu'est-ce que tu chantes là?
Kehs kuh tew shahnt lah?

What are you talking about?

Je sais de quoi je parle.
Zhuh say duh kwah zhuh pahrl.

I know what I'm talking about.

Tu as réponse à tout.
Tew ah ray-pawngs ah too.

You have an answer for everything.

Oublie le jouet un moment.
Oo-blee luh zhoo-ay uhng moh-mawng.

Forget your toy for a moment.

Sers-toi de tes jouets.
Sehr-twah d'tay zhoo-ay.

Use your own toys.

49

CONVERSATIONS

Souviens-toi d'apporter les pastels. Remember to bring your
Soo-v'yehng-twah dah-pawhr-tay lay pahs-tehl. crayons. *

Apporte-moi . . . Bring me...
Ah-pawhrt-mwah...

Viens ici avec moi. Come here with me.
V'yehng ee-see ah-vek mwah.

Tout de suite. Immediately.
Toot sweet.

Va à la salle de bains. Go to the bathroom.
Vah ah lah sall d'bahng.

Passe d'abord. Go first.
Pahss dah-bawhr.

Par ici. Suis-moi. This way. Follow me.
Pahr ee-see. Swee-mwah.

Peux-tu le faire toi-même? Can you do it yourself?
Puh-tew luh fair twah-mehm?

Fais-le sans moi. Do it without me.
Feh-luh sawng mwah.

Ne peux-tu pas le faire toi-même? Can't you do it yourself?
Nuh puh-tew pah luh fair twah-mehm?

Descends aider grand-mère. Go downstairs and help
Day-sawng eh-day grawng-mair. grandma.

Joue / en haut/ en bas/. Play /upstairs/ downstairs/.
Zhoo /awng oh/ awng bah/.

S'il te plait, /sors/ rentre/. Please /go out/ come in/.
Seel tuh pleh, /sawhr/ rawng-tr/.

CONVERSATIONS

Allons! Ah-lohng!	Come on! Let's go!
Vas-y. Vah-zee.	Go ahead.(Go to it.)
Mets la radio. Meh lah rah-d'yoh.	Turn on the radio.
Baisse le baladeur. Behs luh bah-lah-duhr.	Turn down the walkman.
Enlève le casque à écouteurs. Awng-lehv luh kahsk ah ay-koo-tuhr.	Take off the head set. *
Tu me rends folle avec ta musique! Tew muh rohng fohl ah-vek tah mewhz-eek!	You'll drive me crazy with your music!
Eteins la télévision. Ay-tahng lah tay-lay-v'z'yohng.	Turn off the television. *
N'éteins pas la lumière. Nay-tahng pah lah lewh-m'yair.	Don't turn off the light.
Rallume-la. Rah-lewhm-lah.	Turn it on again.
Je ne peux pas trouver mon chemin dans le noir. Zhuh nuh puh pah troo-vay mohng shuh-mahng dawng luh nwawhr.	I can't find my way in the dark.
Appuie sur le bouton. Ah-pwee sewr luh boo-tohng.	Press the switch. *
Ce n'est pas / le tien/ la tienne/. (m/f) Suh neh pah /luh t'yehng/ lah t'yehnn/.	That's not yours.
Ce n'est pas à toi. Suh neh pah-zah twah.	That's not yours.

CONVERSATIONS

Celui-ci est /le tien/ la tienne/. (m/f) Suh-l'wee-see eh /luh t'yehng/ lah t'yehnn/.	This one is yours.
Voilà /le tien/ la tienne/. (m/f) Vwah-lah /luh t'yehng/ lah t'yehnn/.	There is yours.
/Ils/ Elles/ ne sont pas à moi. (m/f) /Eel/ Ell/ nuh sohng pahz-ah mwah.	They're not mine.
Je n'aime pas que tu sortes si tard. Zhuh nehm pah kuh tew sawhrt see tahr.	I don't like you to go out so late.
Ne sois pas si soupçonneux/euse. (m/f) Nuh swah pah see soop-sawng-nuh/ nuhz.	Don't be so suspicious.
Fais-moi donc confiance. Feh-mwah dohng kawng-fee-awngs.	Please trust me.
Ne sois pas en retard. Nuh swah pah-zawng ruh-tahr.	Don't be late.
A quelle heure seras-tu de retour? Ah kell uhr seh-rah-tew d'ruh-toor?	At what time will you be back?
Sois à l'heure! Swah zah luhr!	Be on time!
Pas de plaintes! Pah d'plahngt!	No complaints!

Petit à petit, l'oiseau fait son nid. Every little bit helps.

AIDER chez TOI   HELPING at HOME

Your children are happiest when they are imitating adults in their lives. This includes the work they do. You and your children working together are a natural setting for speaking French together.

Aide-moi à mettre le couvert.
Ehd-mwah ah meh-tr luh koo-vehr.

Help me set the table.

Tu peux mettre la nappe et la serviette.
Tew puh meh-tr lah nahpp ay lah sehr-v'yett.

You can put on the tablecloth and napkins.

Mets le couvert, s'il te plaît.
Meh luh koo-vehr, seel tuh pleh.

Set the table, please.

Dessers la table.
Deh-sehr lah tah-bl.

Clear the table.

Aide-moi à /faire/ essuyer/ la vaisselle.
Ehd-mwah ah/ fair/ eh-swee-yay/ lah veh-sell.

Help me/ wash/ dry/ the dishes.

Aide-moi à /faire le lit/ faire le ménage/ faire le lavage/.
Ehd-mwah ah/ fairluh lee/ fair luh may-nahzh/ fair luh lah-vahzh/.

Help me /make the bed/ clean the house/ do the wash/.   *

HELPING at HOME

As-tu fait ton lit?
Ah-tew feh tohng lee?

Did you make your bed?

Tu me fais travailler.
Tew muh feh trah-vigh-yay.

You make me work.

Maman balaie le plancher.
Mah-mawng bah-lay luh plawng-shay.

Mother's sweeping the floor.

Papa passe l'aspirateur sur le tapis.
Pah-pah pahss lah-spee-rah-tuhr sewr luh tah-pee.

Father vacuums the rug.   *

L'aspirateur fait un drôle de bruit.
Lah-spee-rah-tuhr feh-tuhng drohl d'brwee.

The vacuum cleaner makes a strange noise.

Quelle poussière! Epoussetons.
Kell poo-s'yair! Ay-poos-tohng.

What dust! Let's dust.

Tiens le chiffon à poussière, et frotte.
T'yehng luh shee-fohng ah poos-y'air, ay frawhtt.

Hold the dust cloth and and rub.

Tu n'as pas essuyé ta chambre.
Tew nah pah eh-soo-yay tah shawng-br.

You did not dust your room.

Cette chambre est en désordre! Range-la!
Sett shawng-br eht-awng dayz-awhr-dr! Rawngzh-lah!

This room's a mess! Clean it!

Ta chambre n'a pas été faite.
Tah shawng-br nah pah ay-tay feht.

Your room has not been done.

Aide papa à préparer le dîner.
Ehd pah-pah ah pray-pahr-ay luh dee-nay.

Help father cook dinner.

Maman fait un gâteau.
Mah-mawng feh-tuhng gah-toh.

Mother's baking a cake.   *

Veux-tu m'aider à faire des gâteaux secs?
Vuh-tew meh-day ah fair day gah-toh sehk?

Do you want to help me bake some cookies?

54

HELPING at HOME

Verse la farine.
Vehrs lah fah-reen.

Pour in the flour. *

Ajoute du beurre au sucre.
Ah-zhoot dew buhr oh soo-kr.

Add some butter to the sugar.

Je fouette les oeufs.
Zhuh foo-ett lay-zuh.

I'm beating the eggs.

Je mélange le sucre et le beurre.
Zhuh may-lawnzh luh soo-kr ay luh buhr.

I'm mixing the sugar and the butter. *

Avons-nous besoin de la levure?
Ah-vohng-noo buh-zwahng d'lah luh-vewr?

Do we need baking powder?

On les fait cuire dans le four.
Ohng lay feh k'weer dawng luh foor.

We bake them in the oven.

Mets le compte-minute pour une demie heure.
Meh luh kawngt-mee-newt poor ewn deh-mee uhr.

Set the clock for one-half hour.

Les gâteaux secs sont cuits.
Lay gah-toh sehk sohng kwee.

The cookies are done.

Tu ne peux pas m'aider à repasser.
Tew nuh puh pah meh-day ah ruh-pah-say.

You cannot help me iron.

Tu peux m'aider à/ séparer/ plier/ le linge.
Tew puh meh-day ah/ say-pah-ray/ plee-ay/ luh lahnzh.

You can help me/sort/ fold/ the laundry.

Va étendre le linge sur le fil.
Vah eh-tahng-dr luh lahnzh sewr luh feel.

Go and hang the laundry on the line.

Après le nettoyage, nous pourrons lire une histoire.
Ah-preh luh neht-twah-yahzh, noo poor-ohng leer ewn ees-twahr.

After the cleaning, we can read a story. *

HELPING at HOME

Avant de jouer, il faut que tu ranges ta chambre.
Ah-vawng d'zhoo-ay, eel foh kuh tew rawngzh tah shawng-br.

Before playing, you must straighten your room.

Veux-tu faire les courses?
Vuh-tew fair lay koors?

Do you want to go shopping?

Nous avons besoin d'aller à l'épicerie.
Noo-zah-vohng buh-zwahng dah-lay ah lay-pee-seh-ree.

We need to go to the grocery story.

Tu as besoin de nouveaux vêtements.
Tew ah buh-zwahng d'noo-voh veht-mawng.

You need new clothes.

Il faut que nous enlevions la neige.
Eel foh kuh noo-zawng-leh-v'yohng lah nehzh.

We need to shovel the snow.   *

Veux-tu aller avec moi:
Vuh-tew ah-lay ah-vek mwah:

Do you want to go with me:

   à la boulangerie,
   ah lah boo-lawng-zheh-ree,

   to the bakery,

   à l'épicerie,
   ah lay-pee-seh-ree,

   to the grocer's,

   à la blanchisserie,
   ah lah blawng-shee-seh-ree,

   to the laundry,

   au marché,
   oh mahr-shay,

   to market,

   au grand magasin,
   oh grawng mah-gah-zahng,

   to the department store,

   à la pharmacie,
   ah lah fahr-mah-see,

   to the drug store,

   à la boucherie,
   ah lah boo-sheh-ree,

   to the butcher's,

à la banque,   to the bank,
ah lah bawngk,

à la bibliothèque,   to the library,
ah lah beeb-lee-oh-tehk,

au magasin de chaussures,   to the shoe store,
oh mah-gah-zahng d'shoh-sewhr,

chez le cordonnier?   to the shoemaker?
shay luh kawhr-dawhn-yay?

Aide-moi à tondre la pelouse.   Help me cut the lawn.
Ehd-mwah ah tawng-dr lah puh-looz.

Plante les graines en rangée.   Plant the seeds in a row.
Plawngt lay grahnn awng rawng-zhay.

Il y a tant de mauvaises herbes!   There are so many weeds!
Eel ee ah tawngt-moh-veh-zehrb!

Il faut enlever les mauvaises herbes pour   We need to weed the garden
que les plantes poussent.   so that the plants will grow.   *
Eel foh-tawng-leh-vay lay moh-vay-zehrb poor
kuh lay plawngt poos.

Tu vas m'aider à arroser le jardin?   Will you help me water the
Tew vah meh-day ah ah-roh-zay luh   garden?
zhahr-dahng?

Ne creuse pas trop fort.   Don't dig too hard.
Nuh kruhz pah troh fawhr.

Creuse un petit trou ici.   Dig a little hole here.
Kruhz uhng p'tee troo ee-see.

Fais attention aux chenilles.   Be careful of the caterpillars.   *
Feh-zah-tawng-s'yohng oh shawng-ee-yuh.

Peux-tu ratisser les feuilles?   Can you rake the leaves?
Puh-tew rah-tee-say lay feu-yuh?

HELPING at HOME

Le sol est couvert de feuilles (mortes).
Luh sohl eh koo-vert d'feu-yuh (mohrt).

The ground is covered with (dead) leaves.

Jette les feuilles dans la poubelle.
Zhett lay feu-yuh dawng lah poo-bell.

Throw the leaves into the garbage pail.

N'oublie pas de:
Noo-blee pah duh:

Don't forget to:

   sortir les ordures,
   sawhr-teer layz-ohr-dewhr,

   put out the garbage,

   promener le chien.
   prawh-m'nay luh sh'ehng.

   walk the dog.

C'est à toi de donner à manger au chat.
Seht ah twah d'dawhn-nay ah mawng-zhay oh shah.

It's your turn to feed the cat.

Tu ne peux pas tailler les arbres.
Tew nuh puh pah tigh-yay lay-zahr-br.

You cannot prune the trees.

C'est trop dangereux.
Seh troh dawnzh-ruh.

It's too dangerous.

Au lieu de tailler, tu peux m'aider à faire un wagon.
Oh l'yuh d'tigh-yay, tew puh meh-day ah fair uhng wah-gohng.

Instead of pruning, you can help me make a wagon.   *

Peux-tu sabler ce morceau de bois?
Puh-tew sah-blay suh mawhr-soh d'bwah?

Can you sand this piece of wood?

Scie cette planche en deux.
See sett plawngsh awng duh.

Saw this board in two.   *

Donne-moi le tournevis.
Dawhn-mwah luh toorn-vee.

Give me the screwdriver.

Enfonce ce clou.
Awng-fawngs suh kloo.

Hammer this nail.   *

58

HELPING at HOME

Il faut que je travaille sur notre avion.
Eel foh kuh zhuh trah-vigh-yuh sewr nawh-trah-v'yohng.

I have to work on our plane.

Veux-tu regarder?
Vuh-tew ruh-gahr-day?

Do you want to watch?

Notre bateau a besoin de peinture.
Nawh-tr bah-toh ah buh-zwahng d'pahng-tewhr.

Our boat needs painting.

Veux-tu aller avec moi:
Vuh-tew ah-lay ah-vek mwah:

Do you want to go with me:

à la scierie,
ah lah see-ree,

to the lumber yard,

à la quincaillerie,
ah lah kahng-kigh-yuh-ree,

to the hardware store,

à la pépinière,
ah lah pay-peen-yair,

to the nursery,

à la station service,
ah lah stah-s'yohng sehr-vees,

to the gas station,

à l'aéroport,
ah layr-oh-pawhrt,

to the airport,

au port de plaisance.
oh pawhr d'pleh-zawngs.

to the marina.

Qui n'observe rien n'apprend rien.   Who doesn't observe doesn't learn.

Les CLASSES chez TOI   SCHOOL at HOME

A popular trend is taking place in America where many children and parents are taking charge of their own education. They are doing this at home. For those children who are having classes at home instead of in a school building, these sentences will be useful. Of course, these sentences would apply to a classroom situation as well.

Le car d'école vient de passer!   The school bus just went by!
Luh kahr day-kohl v'yehng d'pah-say!

Il est temps de commencer la classe.   It's time to start class.
Eel eh tawng d'kohng-mawng-say lah klahs.

Où sommes-nous arrêtés/ées (hier)?(m/f)   Where did we stop
Oo sawhm-nooz-ah-reh-tay (ee-yair)?   (yesterday)?

On doit faire le projet des poissons.   There's the fish project
Ohng dwah fair luh proh-zhay day   to do.
pwah-sohng.

Qu'est-ce que c'est?   What is this?
Kehs kuh say?

_____SCHOOL at HOME

Laisse-moi toucher. Lehs-mwah too-shay.	Let me feel.
A qui sont ces crayons? Ah kee sohng say kray-ohng?	Whose pencils are these? *
A qui est ce joujou? Ah kee eh suh zhoo-zhoo?	Whose toy is this?
Je suis content/e d'être chez nous (aujourd'hui). Zhuh swee kawng-tawng/t deh-tr shay noo (oh-zhoor-dwee).	I'm glad we're home (today).
Nous aurons besoin: Nooz-awh-rohng buh-zwahng:	We will need:
de ruban adhésif, d'une agrafeuse, d'rewh-bahn-ah-day-zeef, dewn ah-grah-fuhz,	scotch tape, a stapler,
de ciseaux, de posters. d'see-zoh, d'pohs-tehr.	scissors, posters. *
Il n'y a pas /d'agrafes/ de trombones/. Eel nee ah pah/ dah-graf/ d' trawng-bohn/.	There are no /staples/ paper clips/.
Est-ce qu'on doit étudier la science? Ehs-kohng dwah ay-tewh-d'yay lah s'yahns?	Do we have to do science?
Tu peux lire... Tew puh leer...	You can read...
...pendant que je travaille avec ton frère. ...pawng-dawng kuh zhuh trah-vigh ah-vehk tohng frair.	... while I work with your brother.
Résous 10 fois 22. Ray-zoo dees fwah vahng-duh.	Work out ten times 22.
Veux-tu poser une question? Vuh-tew poh-zay ewn kes-t'yohn?	Do you want to ask a question?

SCHOOL at HOME

Réfléchis avant de répondre.
Ray-flay-shee ah-vawng d'ray-pohng-dr.

Think before answering.

Montre à ta soeur comment faire les
problèmes de mathématiques.
Mawng-trah tah suhr kawh-mawng fair lay
prawh-blehm d'mah-tay-mah-teek.

Show your sister how to
do her math problems. *

Je n'ai pas eu le temps de:
Zhuh nay pah ewh luh tohng duh:

I didn't have time to:

  m'habiller,
  mah-bee-yay,

  get dressed,

  faire mes devoirs,
  fair may duh-vwahr,

  do my homework,

  regarder sur la carte,
  ruh-gahr-day sewr lah kahrt,

  look on the map,

  finir le chapitre.
  fee-neer luh shah-pee-tr.

  finish the chapter.

Maman, la perforeuse est bloquée.
Mah-mawng, lah pehr-fohr-uhz eh bloh-kay.

Mom, the hole punch is stuck.

Il est l'heure de récréation.
Eel eh luhr d'ray-kray-ah-s'yohn.

It's time for recess.

On fait du jardinage.
Ohng feh dew zhahr-dee-nazh.

We'll work in the garden.

Quand nous rentrerons, nous:
Kawng noo rawng-tr-awng, noo:

When we come back, we:

  lirons,
  leer-ohng,

  will read,

  irons en ligne,
  ihr-ohng awhng leehng-yuh,

  will go on-line,

SCHOOL at HOME

enverrons un e-mail à nos cousins, awng-vehr-ohng zuhng ee-mail ah noh koo-zahng,	will send our cousins an E-mail, *
cuirons des biscuits pour oncle Pierre, kweer-ohng day bees-kwee poor awhn-kl P'yehr,	will bake cookies for Uncle Peter,
peindrons un dessin pour papa. pahng-drohng uhng deh-sahng poor pah-pah.	paint a picture for Daddy.
Je suis heureux/ use que nous ne devions pas passer les examens. (m/f) Zhuh sweez-uhr-uh/ uhz kuh noo nuh deh-v'yohn pah pah-say lays-eggs-ah-mawng.	I'm glad we don't have to take exams.
Est-ce que tu as répondu juste? Ehs kuh tew ah ray-pohng-dew zhewst?	Did you get the right answer?
Ces opérations sont justes. Says-oh-pehr-ah-s'yohng sohng zhewst.	These examples are right.
Laquelle de ces réponses est la bonne? Lah-kell d'say ray-pohngs eh lah buhn?	Which of these answers is the right one?
C'est exact. Corrige chaque faute. Set eggs-akt. Koh-reezh shahk foht.	That's correct. Correct every mistake.
Explique-toi plus clairement. Ehks-pleek-twah plewh klair-mawng.	Explain yourself more clearly.
Vois-tu la différence, maintenant? Vwah-tew lah dee-fehr-awngs, mahng-t'nawng?	Do you see the difference, now?
J'ai /raison/ tort/. Zhay /ray-sawng/ tohr/.	I am /right/ wrong/.
Il faut étudier. Eel foht-ay-tewh-d'yay.	We have to study.
As-tu fini tes devoirs? Ah-tew fee-nee tay duh-vwahr?	Did you finish your homework?

SCHOOL at HOME

À bas (les devoirs)!
Ah bah (lay duh-vwahr)!

Down with (homework)!

Tu n'as pas fait tes devoirs.
Tew nah pah feh tay duh-vwahr.

You didn't do your homework.

As-tu fait un peu d'exercice ce matin?
Ah-tew feh unhg puh deggs-ehr-sees suh mah-tahng?

Did you do a little exercise this morning?

Tu ne peux pas écouter la radio pendant que tu fais les devoirs.
Tew nuh puh pah ay-koo-tay lah rah-d'yoh pawng-dawng kuh tew feh lay duh-vwahr.

You cannot listen to the radio while doing homework.

Faisons du football!
Feh-zohng dew foot-bahl!

Let's practice soccer!

Recommence en haut de la page.
Ruh-kawng-mawngs awng oh d'lah pahzh.

Start again at the top of page.

Lis ce texte à haute voix.
Lee suh tehkst ah oht vwah.

Read this text aloud.

Es-tu en train d'écrire le poème?
Eh-tew awng trahng day-kreer luh poh-ehm?

Are you (in the process of) writing the poem?

Tu dois l'apprendre.
Tew dwah lah-prawng-dr.

You've got to learn it.

J'ai besoin de temps supplémentaire pour la musique.
Zhay buh-zwahng d'tawng soo-play-mawng-tair poor lah mewhz-eek.

I need extra time for my music.

Puis-je sauter l'histoire?
Pweezh soh-tay lee-stwahr?

May I skip history?

Passons l'après-midi en plein air.
Pah-sohng lah-preh-mee-dee awng plahng air.

Let's spend the afternoon outdoors.

SCHOOL at HOME

Mon passe-temps favori est le jardinage. Mohng pahs-tawng fah-voh-ree eh luh zhahr-dee-nazh.	My hobby is gardening.
Mes /crayons de couleur/ crayons gras/ ont disparus. May/ kray-ohng d'koo-luhr/ kray-ohng grah/ ohng dees-pah-rewh.	My /colored pencils/ crayons/ are missing.
Quelqu'un les a-t'il trouvés? Kell-kuhng layz-ah-teel troo-vay?	Has anyone found them?
Je n'ai plus de papier. Zhuh nay plew d'pah-p'yay.	I'm out of paper.
Comment avance le travail? Kawh-mawng tah-vawngs luh trah-vigh?	How is the work coming?
Vous avez travaillé beaucoup. Vooz-ah-vay trah-vigh-yay boh-koo.	You (pl) have worked a lot.
Tu as bien fait. La leçon est/ simple / difficile/. Tew ah b'yehng feh. Lah leh-sohng eh/ sahng-pl / dee-fee-seel/.	You did a good job. The lesson is /easy/ difficult/.
/Tu mérites/ Vous méritez/ quelque chose d'agréable. /Tew may-reet/ Voo may-ree-tay/ kell-kuh shohz dah-gray-ah-bl.	You (sing /pl) have earned something nice. *
Range tous ces papiers Rawngzh too say pah-p'yay.	Put away all these papers.
Jette /-le dehors/ les déchets dans la corbeille/. Zhett /-luh deh-ohr/ lay day-sheh dawng lah kawhr-beh-yuh/.	Throw /it out/ the trash in the wastebasket/.
Pouvons-nous avoir congé demain? Poo-vohng-nooz ah-vwahr kawgn-zhay d'mahng?	Can we have off tomorrow?

65

A l'oeuvre on reconnaît l'artisan. You can tell an artist by his work.

La LOUANGE   PRAISE

All the ways to say, "You're tops!" "None better!" "Wonderful, wonderful you!" and many, many more. Use this chapter *often*. You and your child will *love* it.

Quelle belle voix!   What a beautiful voice!
Kell bell vwah!

Tu/ marches/ dessines/ parles/ chantes/   You/ walk/ draw/ speak/
danses/ bien.   sing/ dance/ well.   *
Tew/ mahrsh/ deh-seen/ pahrl/ shahnt/
dawngs/ b'yehng.

Comme tu/ manges/ écris/ nages/ joues/ bien.   How well you/ eat/ write/
Kawhm tew/ mawngzh/ ay-kree/ nahzh/   swim/ play/.
/zhoo/ b'yehng.

Tu es merveilleux/euse. (m/f)   You're wonderful.
Tew eh mehr-veh-yuh/ yuhz.

Tu es brillant/e. (m/f)   You're brilliant.
Tew eh bree-yawng/ t.

PRAISE

Comme tu es mignon/ne. (m/f)	How /sweet/ cute/ you are.
Kawhm tew eh mee-nohng/ nyohnn.	
Comme tu es /jolie/ beau/.	How /pretty/ handsome/ you are.
Kawhm tew eh /zhawh-lee/ boh/.	
Cette robe te va bien.	This dress suits you well.
Sett rawhb tuh vah b'yehng.	
Comme tes yeux sont jolis.	What pretty eyes you have.
Kawhm tay-zyuh sohng zhawh-lee.	
J'aime / tes yeux/ tes mains/ ton ventre/.	I love your /eyes/ hands/ tummy/.
Zhem /tay-zyuh/ tay mahng/ tohng vawng-tr/.	
Quelles jolies ondulations et boucles.	What pretty waves and curls.
Kell zhawh-lee-zawng-dewh-lah-s'yohng ay boo-kl.	
Quel bon enfant!	What a good child! *
Kell bohng awng-fawng!	
Quelle grande fille!	What a big girl!
Kell grawnt fee-yuh!	
Quel bon travail!	What a good job! *
Kell bohng trah-vigh!	
Quel grand garçon!	What a big boy!
Kell grawng gahr-sohng!	
Tu as fait tes premiers pas!	You have taken your first step!
Tew ah feh tay pruh-m'yay pah!	
Que tu es gentil/le! (m/f)	How nice you are!
Kuh tew eh zhawng-tee/ yuh!	
C'est gentil de ta part.	That's nice of you.
Seh zhawng-tee duh tah pahr.	

PRAISE

Tu es de bonne humeur.
Tew ah d'buhn ewh-muhr.

You are in good spirits.

Tu me plaîs. Je t'aime.
Tew muh pleh. Zhuh tehm.

I like you. I love you.

Bravo! Le bébé est debout tout seul.
Brah-voh! Luh bay-bay eh day-boo too suhl.

Well done! Baby is standing all by himself/ herself/.

J'aime bien comment tu joues tout seul sans bruit.
Zhem b'yehng kawh-mawng tew zhoo too suhl sawng brwee.

I like the way you play quietly by yourself.

Tu es gentil/le de me donner la serviette. (m/f)
Tew ay zhawng-tee/ yuh d'muh dawhn-ay lah sehr-v'yett.

You were nice to give me the towel.

Continue à essayer. N'abandonne pas.
Kawng-tee-newh ah eh-say-ay. Nah-bawng-dohng pah.

Keep trying. Don't give up.

Tu vas de mieux en mieux.
Tew vah d'm'yewh awng m'yewh.

You're getting better and better.

J'ai bien apprécié ton aide.
Zhay b'yehng ah-pray-see-yay tohng-nehd.

I certainly liked (appreciated) your help.

Tu as bien nettoyé ta chambre.
Tew ah b'yehng neh-twah-yay tah shawng-br.

You cleaned your room well.

Tu étais patient/e pendant que je parlais au téléphone. (m/f)
Tew ay-tay pah-see-awng/ t pawng-dawng kuh zhuh pahr-lay oh tay-lay-fawhn.

You were patient while I was talking on the phone.   *

Garde le sourire!
Gahrd luh soo-reer!

Keep smiling!

chacun à son goût. To each his own taste.

FAIRE *des* COURSES SHOPPING

This is the area of foreign language conversation which may be unpredictable. When children are young, they enjoy speaking French. However, as they grow more sensitive, they may not wish to appear "different" i.e., speaking a foreign language that others might overhear. Assure them that you understand their feelings. Resume speaking French outside the store or in the car. You might suggest that you and they "play store" at home using French.

Veux-tu faire des courses avec moi? Vuh-tew fair day koors ah-vek mwah?	Do you want to go shopping with me?
Je vais au marché. Zhuh vay oh mahr-shay.	I am going to the market.
J'ai besoin d'acheter ... Zhay buh-zwahng dahsh-tay. . .	I need to buy ...
Il faut rendre ... Eel foh rawng-dr...	I have to return . . . (an item)
Il y a une vente. Eel ee ah ewn vawngt.	There's a sale.

SHOPPING

Je l'ai acheté en solde.
Zhuh lay ahsh-tay awng sawhld.

I bought it on sale.

/Il/ Elle/ me plaît.
/Eel/ Ell/ muh pleh.

I like it.

Qu'est-ce que tu vas acheter avec ton dollar?
Kehs kuh tew vah ahsh-tay ah-vehk tohng dawh-lahr?

What will you buy with your dollar? *

Prenons / l'ascenseur/l'escalier roulant/.
Prawng-nohng/ lah-sawng-suhr/ lehs-kah-lyay roo-lawng/.

Let's take the /elevator/ escalator/.

Tu peux t'asseoir dans le caddy.
Tew puh tah-swahr dawng luh kah-dee.

You can sit in the shopping cart. *

Reste dans le chariot. Reste là.
Rest dawng luh shah-r'oh. Rest lah.

Stay in the shopping cart. Stay there.

Mets les pieds au travers des ouvertures.
Meh lay p'yay oh trah-vehrs day-zoo-vehr-tewhr.

Put your feet through the openings.

Ne marche pas en arrière.
Nuh mahrsh pah awng-nah-r'yair.

Don't walk behind.

Nous ne pouvons pas dépenser trop d'argent.
Noo nuh poo-vohng pah day-pawng-say troh dahr-zhawng.

We cannot spend too much money.

Nous ne pouvons pas acheter ça.
Noo nuh poo-vohng pah-zahsh-tay sah.

We cannot buy that.

C'est (beaucoup) trop cher.
Seh (boh-koo) troh shehr.

That's (much) too expensive.

Peut-être quelque chose de meilleur marché.
Puh-teh-tr kell-kuh shohz d'meh-uhr mahr-shay.

Perhaps something cheaper.

Je suis à court d'argent.
Zhuh sweez ah koor dahr-zhawng.

I'm short of money.

SHOPPING

/Le vendeur/ La vendeuse/ la caisse/ est là-bas.
/Luh vawng-duhr/ Lah vawng-duhz/ lah kehs/ eh lah-bah.

/The salesman/ The saleswoman/ the checkout/ is over there.

Vous désirez?
Voo day-zeer-ay?

Can I help you?

Je regarde seulement.
Zhuh ruh-gahrd suhl-mawng.

I'm only looking.

C'est combien?
Seh kawng-b'yehng?

How much is it?

Combien coûte-t-il?
Kawng-b'yehng koot-teel?

How much does it cost?

Ça fait trois francs cinquante.
Sah feh twah frawng sahng-kant.

That costs three francs fifty centimes.

Cela coûte les yeux de la tête.
Seh-lah koot lay-zyuh d'lah teht.

That costs an arm and a leg.

/Le prix/ La taille/ est marqué/e sur l'étiquette.
/Luh pree/ Lah tigh-yuh/ eh mahr-kay sewr lay-tee-kett.

/The price/ The size/ is marked on the label.

Va-t-on l'acheter?
Vah-tohng lahsh-tay?

Shall we buy it?

Quelle est la taille de ce manteau?
Kell eh lah tigh-yuh d'suh mawng-toh?

What size is this coat?

Fais-moi voir ça.
Feh-mwah vwahr sah.

Let me see that.

Essaie/ -le/ -la/. (m/f)
Eh-say/ -luh/ -lah/.

Try it on.

Il est trop/ étroit/ large/ grand/ petit/.
Eel eh troh /ay-trwah/ lahrzh/ grawng/ p'tee/.

It is too / tight/ loose/ large/ small/.

71

SHOPPING

Il/ elle/ te va très bien. (m/f)   It looks good on you.
Eel/ ell/ tuh vah treh b'yehng.

On a besoin de faire la queue.   We need to stand on line.
Ohng ah buh-zwahng d'fair lah kew.

Compte la monnaie.   Count your change.
Kawngt lah mawh-nay.

Ne touche pas ça.   Don't touch that.
Nuh toosh pah sah.

As-tu besoin d'aller aux lavabos?   Do you need to go to the
Ah-tew buh-zwahng dah-lay oh lah-vah-boh?   washroom?

Plus on est de fous, plus on rit. The more the merrier.

S'AMUSER!   FUN !

If this chapter's pages don't have paint stains, water marks, tire tracks and gum sticking the pages together, you're not getting all there is to wring out of these pages! Be sure to write in some additional sentences and expressions you've learned elsewhere that are appropriate. I've found it helpful to put up sentences and phrases on 3 x 5 cards wherever I need them until the phrase is part of my thinking.

N'as-tu rien à faire?
Nah-tew r'yehng nah fair?

Have you nothing to do?

On n'a rien à faire.
Ohng nah r'yehng ah fair.

We have nothing to do.

Est-ce que tu t'ennuies?
Ehs kuh tew tawng-nwee?

Are you bored?

Viens jouer avec /lui/ elle/.
V'yehng zhoo-ay ah-vek /l'wee/ ell/.

Come play with /him/ her/.

Partage les jouets avec ton frère.
Pahr-tazh lay zhoo-ay ah-vek tohng frair.

Share your toys with your brother.

FUN !

Tu es libre de sortir et jouer. Tew eh lee-br d'sawhr-teer ay zhoo-ay.	You are free to go out and play.
Est-ce que je peux jouer? Ehs kuh zhuh puh zhoo-ay?	Can I play?
Tu peux inviter tes camarades d'école. Tew puh ahng-vee-tay tay kah-mah-rahd day-kohl.	You may invite your school friends.
Demande-leur s'ils veulent jouer: Duh-mawngd-luhr seel vuhl zhoo-ay:	Ask them if they want to play:

    au docteur et à infirmière,   doctor and nurse,   *
    oh dohk-tuhr ay ah ahng-feer-m'yair,

    à la marchande,   store,
    ah lah mahr-shawnd,

    à la maman et au papa,   mother and father,
    ah lah mah-mawng ay oh pah-pah,

    à la poupée,   dolls,   *
    ah lah poo-pay,

    à la marelle,   hopscotch,
    ah lah mahr-ell,

    aux cowboys et aux indiens.   cowboys and indians.
    oh kawh-boy ay awh-zahng-dee-yahng.

Les AVIONS   *AIRPLANES*

Pilote à la tour de contrôle. Pee-lawht ah lah toor d'kawng-trohl.	Pilot to control tower.
Je roule jusqu'à la piste d'envol. Zhuh rool zhews-kah lah peest dawng-vohl.	I'm taxiing.

FUN !

Je décolle. Zhuh day-kawl.	I'm taking off. *
Pouvons-nous atterrir? Poo-vohng-noo ah-teh-reer?	May we land?
Nous n'avons plus d'essence! Noo nah-vohng plewh deh-sawngs!	We're out of gas!
Sur quelle piste atterrit-on? Sewr kell peest ah-teh-ree-tohng?	On which runway may we land?

Les ANIMAUX — *ANIMALS*

Ma trompe est longue; je suis grand; je marche comme ça. Quel animal suis-je? (un éléphant)
Mah trawhnp eh lawhn-guh; zhuh swee grawng; zhuh mahrsh kawhm sah. Kell ah-nee-mahl sweezh? (unhg ay-lay-fawng)

My trunk is long; I'm large; I walk like this. What animal am I? (an elephant)   *

J'ai deux bosses; et je me couche comme ça. Quel animal suis-je? (un chameau)
Zhay duh bawhs; ay zhuh muh koosh kawhm sah. Kell ah-nee-mahl sweezh? (uhng shah-moh)

I have two humps; and I lie down like this. What animal am I? (a camel)   *

J'aboie, et je gronde. Quel animal suis-je? (un chien)
Zhah-bwah, ay zhuh grawngd. Kell ah-nee-mahl sweezh? (uhng sh'ehng)

I bark and growl. What animal am I ? (a dog)   *

Prétendons que nous sommes des kangourous. Sautons.
Pray-tawng-dohng kuh noo sawhm day kawng-goo-roo. Soh-tohng.

Let's pretend we're kangaroos.
Let's hop.   *

Prétendons que nous sommes des coqs. Chantons. Co-co-ri-co!
Pray-tawng-dohng kuh noo sawhm day kawhk. Shahn-tohng. Koh-koh-ree-koh!

Let's pretend we're roosters.
Let's crow. Cock-a-doodle-do!
                *

75

FUN !

Les AUTOS   AUTOMOBILES

Le réservoir est à sec.
Luh ray-zehr-vwahr eh-tah sehk.

The car is out of gas.

Elle ne marche plus.
Ell nuh mahrsh plewh.

It doesn't go any more.

Pourquoi la voiture ne démarre-t-elle pas?
Poor-kwah lah vwah-tewhr nuh day-mahr-tell pah?

Why doesn't the car go?

Je ne peux pas faire marcher cette voiture.
Zhuh nuh puh pah fair mahr-shay sett vwah-tewhr.

I cannot make this car go

Pousse la voiture.
Poos lah vwah-tewhr.

Push the car.

Faites-le plein.
Feht-luh plahng.

Fill 'er up.

Vérifiez l'huile, l'eau et la batterie.
Vay-ree-f'yay l'weel, loh, ay lah bah-teh-ree.

Check the oil, water and battery.

Conduis la voiture dans le garage.
Kawng-dwee lah vwah-tewhr dawng luh gah-rahzh.

Drive the car into the garage.

Papa, puis-je emprunter la voiture?
Pah-pah, pweezh ahng-prunhg-tay lah vwah-tewhr?

Dad, can I borrow the car?

L'ARRIÈRE-COUR   BACK-YARD

Va jouer /dehors/ à l'intérieur/.
Vah zhoo-ay /deh-ohr/ ah lahng-tehr-ee-uhr/.

Go /outside/ inside/ and play.

Joue /dans la cour/dans le bac à sable/.
Zhoo /dawng lah koor/ dawng luh bahk sah-bl/.

Play /in the yard/ in the sandbox/.

_____FUN !

Veux-tu faire des bulles? Vuh-tew fair day bewl?	Do you want to blow bubbles? *
Ne joue pas avec la terre. Nuh zhoo pah ah-vehk lah tair.	Don't play in the dirt.
Ne cueille pas les fleurs. Nuh k'wee pah lay fluhr.	Don't pick the flowers.
Tu peux nager dans la piscine si je suis avec toi. Tew puh nah-zhay dawng lah pee-seen see zhuh swee-zah-vehk twah.	You can swim in the pool if I am with you.
Saute du plongeoir comme je t'ai montré. Soht dew plohng-zhwahr kawhm zhuh tay mawng-tray.	Jump off the diving board as I showed you.
Prends garde en grimpant aux arbres. Prawng gahrd awng grahng-pawng oh-zahr-br.	Be careful climbing trees.
Tous les deux vous pouvez vous asseoir dans le wagon. Too lay duh voo poo-vay voo-zah-swahr dawng luh wah-gohng.	Both of you can sit in the wagon.
Il y a assez de place pour vous deux. Eel ee ah ah-say d'plahs poor voo duh.	There's enough room for two.
Ne sors pas de la cour. Nuh sawhr pah d'lah koor.	Don't leave the yard.

Le BASEBALL   **BASEBALL**

/Attrape/ jette/ frappe/ la balle.   /Catch/ throw/ hit/ the ball.
/Ah-trahp/ zhett/ frapp/ lah bahl.

Tiens la batte derrière toi.   Hold the bat behind you.   *
T'yehng lah batt deh-r'yair twah.

77

FUN !

Ne perds pas la balle de vue.
Nuh pehr pah lah bahl d'vewh.

Keep your eye on the ball.

Va chercher la balle. Cours!
Vah shehr-shay lah bahl. Koor!

Go get the ball. Run!

Brandis! (la batte)
Brawng-dee! (lah batt)

Swing! (the bat)

Tu as manqué! (la balle)
Tew ah mawng-kay! (lah bahl)

You missed! (the ball)

Tu frappes très bien la balle.
Tew frapp treh b'yehng lah bahl.

You are hitting the ball very well.

Le CYCLISME

BICYCLING

Mets le pied sur la pédale.
Meh luh p'yay sewr lah pay-dahl.

Put your foot on the pedal.

Essaie de te tenir en équilibre.
Eh-say d'tuh tuh-neer awng-nay-kee-lee-br.

Try to keep your balance.

Tiens le guidon.
T'yehng luh gee-dohng.

Hold onto the handlebars.

Dirige/ tout droit/ à droite/ à gauche/.
Dee-reezh/too drwah/ ah drwaht/ah gohsh/.

Steer/straight ahead/ right/ left/.   *

Continue à pédaler.
Kawng-tee-newh ah pay-dah-lay.

Keep pedaling.

Tu fais bien du vélo.
Tew feh b'yehng dew vay-loh.

You're riding your bicycle very well.

Sonne la sonnette.
Sawhng lah sawhn-nett.

Ring the bell.

FUN !

Ne fais pas de vélo dans la rue. Il y a trop de circulation.
Nuh feh pah d'vay-loh dawng lah rewh. Eel ee ah troh d'seer-kew-lah-s'yohng.

Don't ride your bicycle in the street. There's too much traffic.

Tu vas trop vite.
Tew vah troh veet.

You're going too fast.

Freine!
Frehn!

Put on the brakes!

T'es-tu blessé/e? (m/f)
Teh-tew bleh-say?

Did you hurt yourself?

Tu te feras mal.
Tew tuh feh-rah mahl.

You'll hurt yourself.

Les JEUX de SOCIÉTÉ   BOARD GAMES   *

A qui le tour?
Ah kee luh toor?

Whose move is it?

C'est à toi (de jouer).
Set ah twah (d'zhoo-ay).

It's your turn (to play).

Ton pion est sur la mauvaise case.
Tohng p'yohng eh sewr lah moh-vehz kahz.

Your piece is in the wrong place.   *

Ce n'est pas jouer franc jeu.
Suh neh pah zhoo-ay frawng zhuh.

That's not playing fair.

Ce n'est pas juste!
Suh neh pah zhewst!

That's not fair.

Avance.
Ah-vawngs.

Move forward.

Reviens à ta place.
Ruh-v'yehng ah tah plahs.

Move backward.

FUN !
_____

Tu gagnes. Tu as gagné. You win. You won.
Tew gahng-yuh. Tew ah gahng-nyay.

Tu perds. Tu as perdu. You lose. You lost.
Tew pehr. Tew ah pehr-dewh.

Les BATEAUX   BOATS

Embarquez! All aboard! (ship)   *
Awng-bahr-kay!

Nous mettons les voiles pour la France. We're sailing to France.
Noo meh-tawng lay vwahl poor lah frawngs.

Le bateau coule! The boat is sinking!
Luh bah-toh kool!

A la mer! Man overboard!
Ah lah mehr!

Quittez le bateau! Abandon ship!
Kee-tay luh bah-toh!

Abaissez les canots de sauvetage! Lower the life boats!   *
Ah-beh-say lay kah-noh d'sohv-tazh!

Nous amarrons. We're docking.
Noo-zah-mahr-ohng.

Nous irons canoter. We'll go for a row.   *
Nooz-eer-ohng kah-noh-tay.

Les PARTIES du CORPS   BODY PARTS

Avec quoi: With what:
Ah-vehk kwah:

  cours-tu, (les jambes)   do you run, (legs)
  koor-tew, (lay zhawngb)

80

_____FUN !

parles-tu, (la bouche) pahrl-tew, (lah boosh)	do you speak, (mouth)
vois-tu, (les yeux) vwah-tew, (lay-zyuh)	do you see, (eyes)
te tiens-tu sur la pointe des pieds? (les orteils) tuh t'yehng-tew sewr lah pwahngt day p'yay ? (lay-zawhr-tay-yuh)	do you stand? (toes)

Le CAMPING   *CAMPING*

Couchons à la belle étoile.   Let's sleep in the open.
Koo-shohng ah lah bell ay-twahl.

Où peut-on dresser la tente?   Where can we set up
Oo puh-tohng dreh-say lah tawngt?   the tent?   *

Cherchons un camping près du lac.   Let's look for a campsite
Shehr-shohng uhng kawng-peeng preh   near the lake.
dewh lahk.

Nous pouvons camper ici.   We can camp here.
Noo poo-vohng kawng-pay ee-see.

COLORIER et COLLER   *COLOR and PASTE*

Laisse-la se servir de tes pastels.   Let her use your crayons.   *
Lehs-lah suh sehr-veer d'tay pah-stehl.

Colore le soleil en jaune.   Color the sun yellow.
Kawh-lawhr luh soh-lay-yuh awng zhohnn.

Peins l'oiseau de la couleur que tu préfères.   Paint the bird the color
Pahng lwah-zoh duh lah koo-luhr kuh tew   you like.
pray-fair.

Dessine une image de papa.   Draw a picture of daddy.
Deh-seen ewn ee-mahzh d'pah-pah.

81

FUN !

Fais un dessin de papa.
Feh-zuhng deh-sahng d'pah-pah.

Draw a picture of daddy.

Dessine le cercle, le triangle, le carré,
comme ça.
Deh-seen luh sehr-kl, luh tree-awng-gl, luh
kah-ray, kawhm sah.

Draw the circle, triangle,
the square like this.   *

Découpe cette image de la revue.
Day-koop sett-tee-mahzh d'lah ruh-vewh.

Cut out this picture from
the magazine.

Colle-la soigneusement sur le papier.
Koll-lah swahng-yuhz-mawng sewr luh
pah-p'yay.

Paste it carefully on
the paper.

Plis le papier /en deux/en quatre/.
Plee luh pah-p'yay /awng duh/awng kahtr/.

Fold the paper /in two/
in four/.

Ne déchire pas le papier.
Nuh day-sheer pah luh pah-p'yay.

Don't tear the paper.

/Roule/ forme/ presse/ la pâte à modeler.
/Rool/ fawhrm/ prehs/ lah paht ah mawhd-lay.

/Roll/ form/ squeeze/ the
clay.

Nettoie les pastels et les papiers.
Neh-twah lay pah-stehl ay lay pah-p'yay

Clean up your crayons
and paper.

Les *ORDINATEURS*   *COMPUTERS*

Allons en ligne.
Ah-lohng zawng leen-yuh.

Let's go on-line.

J'imprime ça
Zhahng-preem sah.

I'll print that out.

Il y a une erreur.
Eel ee ah ewn ehr-ruhr.

There's an error.

J'ai oublié le mot de passe.
Zhay oo-bl'yay luh moh d'pahs.

I forgot my password.

On peut chercher l'information ou feuilleter.
Ohng puh shehr-shay lahng-fohr-mah-s'yohn oo feu-yuh-tay.

We can search for information or browse.

Envoyons une télécopie.
Awng-vwah-yohng ewn tay-lay-koh-pee.

Let's send a fax.

Les POUPÉES

DOLLS

Donne à manger à la poupée.
Dawhn ah mawng-zhay ah lah poo-pay.

Feed the doll.

Sers-lui une bonne tasse de thé.
Sehr-l'wee ewn buhn tahs d'tay.

Give/ him/ her/ a nice cup of tea.

Habille la poupée.
Ah-bee-yuh lah poo-pay.

Dress the doll.   *

Allonge-la doucement.
Ah-lohngzh-lah doos-mawng.

Lay her down gently.

Ne la traine pas sur le plancher.
Nuh lah trehn pah sewr luh plawng-shay.

Don't drag her on the floor.

Prends soin de l'ours en peluche.
Prawng swahng d'loors awng peh-loosh.

Take good care of the teddy bear.

Ne lui donne pas la fessée.
Nuh l'wee dawhn pah lah feh-say.

Don't spank her so hard.

Comment s'appelle la poupée?
Kawh-mawng sah-pell lah poo-pay?

What is the doll's name?

Les VOITURES de POMPIERS

FIRE ENGINES

Au secours! Au feu!
Oh suh-koor! Oh fuh!

Help! Fire!

Envoyez chercher les voitures de pompiers!
Awng-vwah-yay shehr-shay lay vwah-tewhr duh pohng-p'yay!

Send for the fire engines!

FUN !

Sonnez la sirène!   Sound the siren!
Sawhng-ay lah see-rehn!

JEU à la QUEUE LEU LEU   *FOLLOW-the-LEADER*

Je suis le chef. Imite-moi.   I'm the leader. Do what I do.
Zhuh swee luh shef. Ee-meet-mwah.

CACHE-CACHE   *HIDE-and-SEEK*

Jouons à cache-cache.   Let's play hide and seek.
Zhoo-ohng ah kash-kash.

Va te cacher (pendant que je compte jusqu'à dix).   Go hide (while I count up
Vah tuh kah-shay (pawng-dawng kuh zhuh   to ten).
kawngt zhews-kah dees).

Où es-tu?   Where are you?
Oo eh-tew?

Où suis-je? (Cache-cache)   Where am I?
Oo swee-zh? (kash-kash)   (Hide-and-seek)

Je ne sais pas où tu es caché/e. (m/f)   I don't know where you
Zhuh nuh say pah oo tew eh kah-shay.   are hidden.

Je vais t'attraper.   I'm going to get you.
Zhuh vay tah-trah-pay.   (chasing)

<<Attrapé!>>   "Gotcha!"
<<Ah-trah-pay!>>

Les OBSTACLES   *OBSTACLE GAMES*

Va là-bas: Go over there:
Vah lah-bah:

    au travers du cerceau,   through the hoop,
    oh trah-vehrs dew sehr-soh,

autour du cabinet, oh-toor dew kah-bee-neh,	around the cabinet,
sous la table, soo lah tah-bl,	under the table,
à côté de la chaise. ah koh-tay d'lah shehz.	beside the chair.
Mets-toi debout derrière moi, Meh-twah day-boo deh-r'yair mwah,	Stand behind me,
devant le canapé. duh-vawng luh kah-nah-pay.	in front of the couch.

Le PARC de JEUX   *PLAYGROUND*

Balance-toi! Mais ne te balance pas trop haut. Bah-lawngs-twah! Meh nuh tuh bah-lawngs pah troh oh.	Swing! But don't swing too high. *
Ne saute pas de la balançoire. Nuh soht pah d'lah bal-lawng-swahr.	Don't jump off the swing.
Ne te mets pas debout sur la balançoire. Nuh tuh meh pah day-boo sewr lah bah-lawng-swahr.	Don't stand on the swing.
Je te pousserai gentiment. Zhuh tuh poos-ray zhawng-tee-mawng.	I'll push you gently.
Ne ferme pas les yeux. Nuh fehrm pah lay-zyuh.	Don't close your eyes.
Tiens le toboggan. T'yehng luh toh-boh-gawng.	Hold onto the slide. *
Descends en glissant doucement. Day-sawng awng glee-sawng doos-mawng.	Slide down easily.

FUN !

Le cerf-volant tombe; il n'y a pas assez de vent.
Luh sehr--voh-lawng tawngb; eel nee ah pah ah-say d'vawng.

The kite is falling; there's not enough wind. *

Tiens la queue.
T'yehng lah kewh.

Hold onto the tail.

Veux-tu sauter à la corde ou jouer à la toupie?
Vuh-tew soh-tay ah lah kawhrd oo zhoo-ay ah lah too-pee?

Do you want to jump rope or play with the top?

Je veux faire du jogging.
Zhuh vuh fair dew zhoh-geeng.

I want to go jogging.

Quelle hauteur peux-tu sauter?
Kell oh-tuhr puh-tew soh-tay?

How high can you jump?

Jusqu'où peux-tu courir?
Zhews-koo puh-tew koo-reer?

How far can you run?

Lance les billes dans le cercle.
Lawngs lay bee-yuh dawng luh sehr-kl.

Shoot the marbles into the circle.

Gonfle le ballon. Il se dégonfle.
Gawng-fl luh bah-lawng. Eel suh day-gawng-fl.

Blow up the balloon. Air is leaking from it. *

Je mène! Tu es /le dernier/ la dernière/. (m/f)
Zhuh mehn! Tew eh /luh dehrn-yay/ lah dehrn-yair/.

I'm in the lead! You're last.

Les CASSE-TÊTES

PUZZLES

Mettons ici ce morceau du casse-tête.
Meh-tawng ee-see suh mawhr-soh dew kass-teht.

Let's put this piece of the puzzle here. *

Ce morceau ne va pas bien.
Suh mawhr-soh nuh vah pah b'yehng.

This piece doesn't fit.

86

FUN !

Il manque quel morceau?　　　　　　　What piece is missing?
Eel mawngk kell mawhr-soh?

Le PATINAGE　　　　　　　　　　　SKATING

Mes patins sont émoussés. Il faut les aiguiser.　My skates are dull. They
May pah-tahng sohng tay-moo-say. Eel foh　need sharpening.　　*
lay-zay-gee-zay.

Tiens-toi bien à moi. Je t'aiderai à patiner.　Hold onto me. I'll help
T'yehng-twah b'yehng ah mwah. Zhuh teh-　you skate.
d'ray ah pah-tee-nay.

Lève le pied droit.　　　　　　　　　　Lift your right foot.
Lehv luh p'yay drwah.

Pousse avec ton pied gauche.　　　　　　Push with your left foot.
Poos ah-vehk tohng p'yay gohsh.

Patine tout autour de la patinoire.　　　　Skate around the rink.
Pah-teen toot-oh-toor d'lah pah-tee-nwahr.

Tu es prêt/e à patiner en arrière. (m/f)　　You're ready to skate
Tew eh preh/ t ah pah-tee-nay awng-nah-r'yair.　backwards.

Patine seulement dans l'allée.　　　　　Skate only in the driveway.
Pah-teen suhl-mawng dawng lah-lay.

Le FOOTBALL　　　　　　　　　　　SOCCER

Ne touche pas la balle avec les mains.　　Don't touch the ball with
Nuh toosh pah lah bahl ah-vehk lay mahng.　your hands.

Lance la balle au but. Allez!　　　　　Kick the ball into the goal.
Lawngs lah bahl oh bewht. Ah-lay!　　　Go!

La balle est allée droit au but.　　　　The ball went straight into
Lah bahl eht ah-lay dwaht-oh bewht.　　the goal.

Shoote! Tu as marqué un but!　　　　　Shoot! You have scored
Shoot! Tew ah mahr-kay uhng bewht!　　a goal!　　　　　　*

FUN !

Les TRAINS — TRAINS *

En voiture!
Awng vwah-tewhr!

All aboard! (train)

Les billets, s'il vous plait.
Lay bee-yay, seel voo pleh.

Tickets, please.

Quel est le prix de la course?
Kell eh luh pree d'lah koors?

How much is the fare?

Quand arrive-t-on à New York?
Kawng-tah-reev-tohng ah New York?

When do we arrive in New York?

Les CAMIONS — TRUCKS

Délivres-tu de l'huile dans le camion citerne?
Day-lee-vr-tew d'l'weel dawng luh kah-mee-yohng see-tehrn?

Are you delivering oil in your oil truck?

Ce n'est pas un camion citerne;
c'est un wagon à bestiaux.
Suh neh pah-zuhng kah-mee-yohng see-tehrn;
seh-tuhng wah-gohng ah behs-tyoh.

This isn't an oil truck; this is a cattle truck.

Je charge mon camion avec du sable.
Zhuh shahrzh mohng kah-mee-ohng ah-vehk dew sah-bl.

I'm loading my truck with sand. *

POT-POURRI — MISCELLANEOUS

Cou-Cou!
Koo-Koo!

Peek-a-boo!

Qui est-ce?
Kee ehs?

Guess who?

Agite le hochet.
Ah-zheet luh oh-sheh.

Shake the rattle.

_____FUN !

Empile les cubes les uns sur les autres. Awng-peel lay kewb lay-zuhng sewr lay-zoh-tr.	Stack the blocks on top of each other.
Ne les démolis pas! Nuh lay day-mawh-lee pah!	Don't knock them down!
Où est le mouchoir? (Cache-mouchoir) Oo eh luh moo-shwahr? (Kash-moo-shwahr)	Where is the handkerchief? (Hide-the-handkerchief)
Vas-tu jouer à colin-maillard? Vah-tew zhoo-ay ah koh-lahng-migh-yahr?	Are you going to play blindman's buff?
Regarde par la fenêtre. Ruh-gahrd pahr lah fuh-neh-tr.	Look out of the window.
Que vois-tu? Kuh vwah-tew?	What do you see?
Je vois avec mes yeux quelque chose de brun et grand. (un arbre) Zhuh vwah ah-vehk may-zyuh kell-kuh shohz d'bruhng ay grawng. (uhng-nahr-br)	I spy with my little eye something that is brown and tall. (a tree)
Roule/ le cerceau/ la balle/. Rool/ luh sehr-soh/ lah bahl/.	Roll the/ hoop/ ball/ .
Veux-tu jouer/au jeu des carrés/ aux cartes/ avec moi? Vuh-tew zhoo-ay/oh zhuh day kah-ray/ oh kahrt/ ah-vehk mwah?	Do you want to play/ ticktacktoe/ cards/ with me?
Frappe des mains. Frapp day mahng.	Clap your hands.
Tape des pieds. Tahp day p'yay.	Tap your feet.

FIN de JOUER — END of PLAY

Arrête de jouer. Range tes affaires. Ah-reht d'zhoo-ay. Rawngzh teh-zah-fair.	Stop playing. Tidy up your things.

FUN !

Il est l'heure de dîner. Eel eh luhr d'dee-nay.	It's time for dinner.
Range tous les jouets dans la boîte à jouets. Rawngzh too lay zhoo-eh dawng lah bwaht ah zhoo-eh.	Put all your toys back in the toy box.
As-tu rangé tes jouets? Ah-tew rawng-zhay tay zhoo-ay?	Have you put all your toys away?
Tu ne /le/la/les/ range jamais. Tew nuh/ luh/ lah/ lay/ rawngzh zhah-may.	You never put /it (m)/ it (f)/ them/ away.
Je range toujours tout. Zhuh rawngzh too-zhoor too.	I always put everything away.
Où as-tu laissé ton clown? Oo ah-tew lehs-ay tohng kloon?	Where did you leave your clown?
Veux-tu faire une promenade? Vuh-tew fair ewn prawg-m'nahd?	Do you want to go for a walk?
Tiens ma main. T'yehng mah mahng.	Take (Hold) my hand.
Préfères-tu faire une promenade en voiture? Pray-fair-tew fair ewn prawg-m'nahd awng vwah-tewhr?	Would you prefer to take a ride?
Tiens-toi à la voiture d'enfant. T'yehng-twah ah lah vwah-tewhr dawng-fawng.	Hold onto the carriage.
Tu donnes ta langue au chat? Tew dawhn tah lahng oh shat?	Do you give up?

C'est dans le besoin qu'on connaît les amis. A friend in need is a friend indeed.

SAMEDI APRÈS-MIDI   SATURDAY AFTERNOON

The opportunities for using French on Saturdays are unlimited. Saturdays were made for French! Chores to be done using French, visits to friends and relatives using French, shopping, outings, sports. The list is endless as you can see.

Allons /au cinéma/ à la galerie marchande/. Ah-lohng/ zoh see-nay-mah/ zah lah gah-leh-ree mahr-shawngd/.	Let's go/ to the movies/ to the mall/.
J'adore les dessins animés. Zhah-dohr lay deh-sahng-zah-nee-may.	I love cartoons.
Marie, peut-elle venir avec nous? Mah-ree, puh-tell vuh-neer ah-vehk noo?	Can Mary come with us?
J'aimerais mieux aller au parc de jeux. Zheh-meh-ray m'yewh ah-lay oh pahrk d'zhoo.	I'd rather go to the playground.
C'est plus amusant. Seh plewhz-ah-mewhz-awng.	It's more fun.
Est-ce que je peux sortir pour jouer? Ehs kuh zhuh puh sawhr-teer poor zhoo-ay?	Can I go out and play?

SATURDAY AFTERNOON

Je sors. Zhuh sawhr.	I'm going out.
As-tu fini tes travaux domestiques? Ah-tew fee-nee tay trah-voh doh-mehs-teek?	Are you finished with your chores?
Il y a une exposition /de trains/ de fleurs/. Eel-ee-ah ewn ehks-poh-zee-s'yohn /d'trahng/ d'fluhr/.	There's a /train/ flower/ show.
Il y a une pièce à l'école. Eel ee ah ewn p'yehs ah lay-kohl.	There is a school play.
Il y a un spectacle de marionnettes à la bibliothèque. Eel ee ah uhng speh-tah-kl d'mah-ree-oh-nett ah lah bee-blee-oh-tehk.	There's a puppet show at the library.
Il y a une exposition de voitures au colisée. Eel ee ah ewn ehks-poh-zee-s'yohn d'vwah-tewhr oh koh-lee-say.	There's a car show at the coliseum.
On va / en métro/ en bus/. Ohng vah /awng may-troh/ awng bews/.	We'll go / by subway/ by bus/.
Peut-on dîner en ville? Puh-tohng dee-nay awng veel?	Can we eat out?
Je veux dîner dans un restaurant (à service rapide). Zhuh vuh dee-nay dawng-zuhng rehs-toh-rawng (ah sehr-vees rah-peed).	I want to eat in a restaurant/ (fast food place).
Tu as rendez-vous chez le dentiste. Tew ah rawng-day-voo shay luh dawng-teest.	You have an appointment at the dentist's.
L'appareil dentaire a besoin d'être ajusté. Lah-pah-ray-yuh dawng-tair ah buh-zwahng deh-tr ah-zhoos-tay.	Your braces need to be adjusted.

SATURDAY AFTERNOON

Non! Tu ne peux pas teindre en rouge les cheveux! / No, you can't dye your hair red!
Nohng! Tew nuh puh pah tahng-drawng roozh lay shuh-vuh!

Entre dans la voiture! On va se promener en voiture. / Get in the car! We'll go for a ride.
Awng-tr dawng lah vwah-tewhr! Ohng vah suh prawh-m'nay awng vwah-tewhr.

Téléphone_____. Nous: / Call up_____. We:
Tay-lay-fohng_____. Noo:

ferons de la planche à roulettes, / will go skateboarding, *
feh-rohng d'lah plawngsh ah roo-lett,

patinerons /à roulettes/ en ligne/. / will go /roller skating/ roller blading/.
pah-tee-neh-rohng /ah roo-lett/ awng leen-yuh/.

Le delta-plane serait amusant. / Hang gliding would be fun.
Luh dehl-tah-plahn seh-ray ah-mewhz-awng.

Ecoutons mon nouveau CD. / Let's listen to my new CD.
Ay-koo-tohng mohng noo-voh say-day.

Je préfère aller à la pêche. / I would rather go fishing. *
Zhuh pray-fair ah-lay ah lah pehsh.

Nous avons l'amorce, les hameçons et le filet. / We've got the bait, the hooks and the net.
Nooz-ah-vohng lah-mohrs, layz-ahm-sohng ay luh fee-lay.

Tu as oublié la canne à pêche. / You forgot the fishing rod.
Tew ah oo-bl'yay lah kahnn ah pehsh.

Aimerais-tu aller à la pêche? / Would you like to go fishing?
Ehm-ray-tew ah-lay ah lah pehsh?

Où se trouve la bonne pêche? / Where is a good spot for fishing?
Oo suh troov lah buhn pehsh?

SATURDAY AFTERNOON

J'ai attrapé un poisson!   I caught a fish!
Zhay ah-trah-pay uhng pwah-sohng!

La ligne de pêche est saisi au fond.   The line is caught on the
Lah leeng d'pehsh eh say-zee oh fohng.   bottom.

Peut-on pêcher à marée basse?   Can we fish at low tide?
Puh-tohng peh-shay ah mah-ray bahss?

Peut-on finir la cabane (construite dans un arbre)?   Can we finish the tree house?
Puh-tohng fee-neer lah kah-bahn (kawng-strweet
dawng-zuhng ah-br)?

Je recueillerai le marteau, les clous, la scie   I'll get the hammer, nails,
et les planches.   the saw and boards.
Zhuh reh-kuh-yuh-ray luh mahr-toh, lay kloo,
la see ay lay plawngsh.

Rencontre-moi à l'arrière-cour.   Meet me in the back-yard.
Rawng-kawng-tr-mwah ah lah-r'yehr-koor.

Allons au grenier.   Let's go to the attic.
Ah-lohng-zoh grawng-nyay.

Regardons le match de football (à la   Let's watch the soccer match
télévision).   (on TV).
Ruh-gahr-dohng luh match d'foot-bahl
(ah lah tay-lay-v'z'yohng).

Lisons des bandes dessinées.   Let's read comic-books.
Lee-zohng day bahnd deh-see-nay.

Allons /à la plage/ au lac/.   Let's go /to the beach/ to
Ah-lohngz /ah lah plahzh/ oh lahk/.   the lake/.

Allons /au rivage/ à la piscine/.   Let's go /to the shore/ to
Ah-lohngz/ oh ree-vahzh/ ah lah pee-seen/.   the pool/.

Allons nager.   Let's go swimming.
Ah-lohng nah-zhay.

SATURDAY AFTERNOON

Allons faire du ski nautique.
Ah-lohng fair dew skee noh-teek.

J'apporterai les serviettes,
Zhah-pohr-t'ray lay sehr-v'yett,

   le parasol,
   luh pah-rah-sohl,

   le transat, le seau et la pelle.
   luh trahn-zah, luh soh ay lah pell.

/Le ciel/ L'eau/ est clair/e.
/Luh s'yehl/ Loh/ eh klair.

L'eau est agréable, n'est-ce pas?
Loh eh-tah-gray-ah-bl, nehs pah?

La mer est / houleuse/ calme/ chaude/ froide/.
Lah mehr eh /too-luhz/ kahlm/ shohd/ frwahd/.

Etends la couverture/ au soleil/ à l'ombre/.
Ay-tawng lah koo-vehr-tewhr/ oh soh-lay-yuh/ ah lohng-br.

Pourquoi tu ne te couches pas sur la couverture?
Poor-kwah tew nuh tuh koosh pah sewr lah koo-vehr-tewhr?

On peut partager le matelas pneumatique.
Ohng puh pahr-tah-zhay luh mah-t'lah p'newh-mah-teek.

Tu ne peux pas rentrer dans l'eau.
Tew nuh puh pah rawng-tray dawng loh.

Tu viens de déjeuner!
Tew v'yehng d'day-zhuh-nay!

Il y a des méduses ici!
Eel ee ah day may-dewhz ee-see!

Let's go water-skiing.

I'll bring the towels,

   the umbrella,

   the beach chair, the pail
   and shovel.   *

The /sky/ water/ is clear.

Doesn't the water feel nice?

The sea is / rough/ calm/ warm/ cold/.

Spread the blanket /in the sun /in the shade/.

Why don't you lie down on the blanket?

We can share the air mattress.

You aren't allowed back in the water.

You have just eaten lunch!

There are jelly fish here!

95

SATURDAY AFTERNOON

Il est tard. Eel eh tahr.	It's getting late.
Pourquoi ne ramasses-tu pas de coquillages? Poor-kwah nuh rah-mahss-tew pah duh koh-kee-yahzh?	Why don't you look for seashells? *
Bâtis un château de sable. Bah-tee uhng shah-toh d'sah-bl.	Build a sand castle. *
Dessine des images sur le sable. Deh-seen dayz-ee-mahzh sewr luh sah-bl.	Draw pictures on the sand.
Regarde les oiseaux/ atterrir/ voler/. Ruh-gahrd layz-wah-zoh/ ah-tehr-reer/ voh-lay/.	Watch the birds/ land/ fly/.
Cet hors-bord est tout près de la bouée. Seht awhr-bawhr eh too preh d'lah boo-ay.	That speed boat is very close to the buoy. *
Surveille ta soeur! Sewr-vay-yuh tah suhr!	Keep an eye on your sister!
Tu as attrapé un coup de soleil. Tew ah ah-trah-pay uhng koot-soh-lay-yuh.	You are sunburnt.
Où est le lait solaire? Oo eh luh lay soh-lair?	Where is the suntan lotion?
Où sont tes lunettes de soleil? Oo sohng tay lewh-nett d'soh-lay-yuh?	Where are your sun-glasses? *
Où sont le déjeuner et les boissons? Oo sohng luh day-zhuh-nay ay lay bwah-sohng?	Where are the lunch and the drinks?
Quelle bonne journée pour nager. Kell buhn zhoor-nay poor nah-zhay.	What a beautiful day for swimming.
Quelle bonne journée pour faire du ski. Kell buhn zhoor-nay poor fair dew skee.	What a beautiful day for skiing.

SATURDAY AFTERNOON

Je veux faire de la luge. Zhuh vuh fair d'lah lewhzh.	I want to go sledding.
Il ne faut pas louer: Eel nuh foh pah loo-ay:	We don't need to rent:
des skis, day skee,	the skis,
des bâtons de ski, day bah-tohng d'skee,	the ski poles,
des chaussures. day show-sewr.	the boots.
Nous avons notre propre équipement. Nooz-ah-vohng nawh-tr prawh-pr ay-keep-mawng.	We have our own equipment.
La neige est /trop molle/ trop dure/. Lah nehzh eh /troh mawhll/ troh dewhr/.	The snow is /too soft/ too hard/.
Combien coûtent les billets pour le remonte-pente? Kawng-b'yehng koot lay bee-yay poor luh ruh-mawngt-pawngt?	How much are chairlift tickets?
Où est le guichet? Oo eh luh guee-sheh?	Where is the ticket office?
Ne va pas au sommet! Nuh vah pah oh soh-meh!	Don't go to the top!
La colline est trop raide. Lah kawh-leen eh troh rehd.	The hill is too steep.
C'est dangereux! Seh dawng-zhuh-ruh!	That's dangerous!
Ne fais pas du ski trop vite! Nuh feh pah dew skee troh veet!	Don't ski so fast! *

SATURDAY AFTERNOON

Quelle forme!   What form!
Kell fawhrm!

As-tu /faim/ froid/?   Are you / hungry/ cold/?
Ah-tew /fahng/ frwah/?

J'ai /faim/ froid/.   I am /hungry/cold/.
Zhay /fahng/ frwah/.

Es-tu fatigué/e? (m/f)   Are you tired?
Eh-tew fah-tee-gay/?

Entrons: Let's go inside:
Awng-trohng:

   pour se reposer,   in order to rest,
   poor suh ruh-poh-zay,

   pour manger,   in order to eat,
   poor mawng-zhay,

   pour nous réchauffer.   in order to warm up.
   poor noo ray-shoh-fay.

Il fait bon et chaud ici.   It's pleasant and warm here.
Eel feh bohng ay shoh ee-see.

Prenons des photos! Souriez!   Let's take some photos!
Prawng-nohng day foh-toh! Soo-r'eh!   Smile!

Je fais des anges dans la neige.   I'm making angels in the
Zhuh feh dayz ahngzh dawng lah nehzh.   snow.

Quand part-on?   When are we leaving?
Kawng pahr-tohng?

Jusqu'où allons-nous?   How far are we going?
Zhews-koo ahl-lohng-noo?

SATURDAY AFTERNOON

Quand est-ce qu'on arrive?
Kawngt ehs-kohng nah-reev?

When will we get there?

Nous y serons en moins de cinq minutes.
Nooz-ee seh-rohng awng mwahng duh sahngk mee-noot.

We'll be there within five minutes.

Il est l'heure de partir.
Eel eh luhr d'pahr-teer.

It is time to go.

Y a-t-il moyen de:
Ee-ah-teel mwah-ehng duh:

Is there any way of:

   partir plus tard,
   pahr-teer plewh tahr,

   leaving later,

   revenir encore?
   ruh-vuh-neer awng-kohr?

   coming back again?

Il y aura beaucoup de circulation.
Eel ee awh-rah boh-koo d'seer-kew-lah-s'yohng.

There will be a lot of traffic.

Ramasse tes affaires.
Rah-mahs tayz-ah-fair.

Be sure that you have everything.

Est-ce que tu t'es amusé/e? (m/f)
Ehs kuh tew teh ah-mewhz-ay?

Did you have a good time?

Je me suis amusé/e. (m/f)
Zhuh muh sweez-ah-mewhz-ay.

I had a good time.

Tous les goûts sont dans la nature. It takes all kinds.

Les EXCLAMATIONS / EXCLAMATIONS

Ha! Formidable!
Ah! Fawhr-mee-dah-bl!
Ah! Wow!

Aïe! Pouf! Zut!
Ay! Poof! Zewht!
Ouch! Whoops! Darn!

Oh, mon Dieu!
Oh, mawng Dyuh!
Oh, dear!

Je suis triste.
Zhuh swee treest.
I'm sad.

Tu parais triste.
Tew pah-ray treest.
You look sad.

Je suis heureux/euse! (m/f)
Zhuh swee-zuhr-uh/ uhz!
I'm glad!

Nous sommes heureux que tu aies gagné!
Noo sawhm-zuhr-uh kuh tew ay gah-nyay!
We're glad that you won!

EXCLAMATIONS

Au secours! Attention! Oh suh-koor! Ah-tawng-s'yohng!	Help! Look out!
On te l'a dit... Ohng tuh lah dee...	You were told...
As-tu fait comme je te l'ai dit? Ah-tew feh kawhm zhuh tuh lay dee?	Did you do as I told you?
Pourquoi me regardes-tu comme ça? Poor-kwah muh ruh-gahrd-tew kawhm sah?	Why are you looking at me like that?
Fais ce qu'on te dit. Feh s'kohng tuh dee.	Do as you are told.
Je ne peux pas. Tu peux. Zhuh nuh puh pah. Tew puh.	I can't. You can.
Qui te l'a dit? Kee tuh lah dee?	Who told you so?
A qui la faute? Ah kee lah foht?	Whose fault is it?
Je suis désolé/e. (m/f) C'est ma faute. Zhuh swee dayz-oh-lay. Seh mah foht.	I'm sorry. It's my fault.

(or)

Tu es en tort. Tew eh awng tohr.	It is your fault.
Je regrette ce que j'ai fait. Zhuh ruh-grett s'kuh zhay feh.	I'm sorry for what I did.
Faisons la paix. Feh-zohng lah pay.	Let's make peace. (Let's kiss and make up.)
Je regrette que tu sois tombé/e. (m/f) Zhuh ruh-grett kuh tew swah tawng-bay.	I'm sorry that you fell.

EXCLAMATIONS

Alors!   Well now!
Ah-lawhr!

N'est-ce pas? Hein?   Isn't that so?
Nehs-pah ? Ahng?

N'importe!   Who cares! I don't care!
Nahng-pawhrt!

Ça ne fait rien.   It doesn't matter.
Sah nuh feh r'yehng.

Tout le monde le fait.   Everybody does it.
Too luh mohnd luh feh.

Es-tu /fou/ folle/? (m/f)   Are you crazy?
Eh-tew /foo/ fohl/?

Je m'en moque!   I don't care!
Zhuh mawng mohk!

Tu ne peux pas faire à ta tête.   You can not have
Tew nuh puh pah fair ah tah teht.   your own way.

Cela peut attendre!   That can wait!
Suh-lah puht ah-tawng-dr!

Qui sait?   Who knows?
Kee say?

Tout peut arriver.   Anything can happen.
Too puh-tahr-ree-vay.

Ce sera bientôt fini.   It will soon be over.
Suh seh-rah b'yehng-toh fee-nee.

Holà!   Go easy!
Oh-lah!

EXCLAMATIONS

D'accord. Entendu!
Dah-kawhr. Awng-tawng-dew!
    O. K. All right!

Sans rancune!
Sawng rawng-kewn!
    No hard feelings!

Bien sûr! C'est ça.
B'yehng sewr! Seh sah.
    Of course! That's right.

Mais non!
Meh nohng!
    Of course not!

N'en dis pas plus!
Nawng dee pah plewh!
    Say no more!

Sans doute! C'est entendu!
Sawng doot! Set-awng-tawng-dew!
    Certainly! Sure!

Sans faute!
Sawng foht!
    Without fail!

Tu pourrais faire mieux.
Tew poor-ay fair m'yewh.
    You could do better.

Je ferai de mon mieux.
Zhuh feh-ray d'mohng m'yewh.
    I'll do my best.

Je le ferai moi-même.
Zhuh luh feh-ray mwah-mehm.
    I'll do it myself.

C'est facile comme tout.
Seh fah-seel kawhm too.
    It's as easy as anything.

On s'y fait au bout de quelque temps.
Ohng see feh oh boo d'kell-kuh tawng.
    It grows on you after a while.

Que c'est /intéressant/ drôle/!
Kuh seh /tahng-tehr-ess-sawng/drohl!
    How /interesting/ funny/!

EXCLAMATIONS

Quelle bêtise!   What nonsense!
Kell beh-teez!

Quelle chance!   What luck!
Kell shawngs!

/J'ai/ Tu as/ de la chance!   /I'm/ You're/ lucky!   *
/Zhay/ Tew ah/ d'lah shawngs!

Cela n'arrive qu'à moi!   It's just my luck!
Suh-lah nah-reev kah mwah!

Que c'est effroyable!   How awful!
Kuh set-eh-fwah-yah-bl!

Tant pis! Quel dommage!   Too bad! What a pity!
Tawng pee! Kell doh-mahzh!

Tu t'y habitueras.   You'll get used to it.
Tew tee ah-bee-t'yewh-rah.

Que c'est rare!   How unusual!
Kuh seh rahr!

C'est extraordinaire!   That's extraordinary!
Set-ehks-trawh-dee-nair!

Regarde-moi, Maman!   Look at me, Mom!
Ruh-gahrd-mwah, mah-mawng!

Que c'est agréable!   How kind/ nice!
Kuh set-ah-gray-ah-bl!

Merveilleux!   Marvelous! Wonderful!
Mehr-veh-yuh!

Quelle blague!   What a joke!
Kell blahg!

EXCLAMATIONS

C'était pour rire! / Say-tay poor reer! — It was a joke!

/Je pense/ J'espère /que/oui/ non/! / /Zhuh pawngs/ Zheh-spair /kuh/ wee/ nohng/! — /I think/ I hope /so/ not/!

Ça va sans dire. / Sah vah sawng deer. — That goes without saying.

Je dirais que oui! / Zhuh dee-ray kuh wee! — I should say so!

Décide-toi. / Day-seed-twah. — Make up your mind.

Je suis sérieux/euse! (m/f) / Zhuh swee say-ree-uh/ uhz/! — I'm serious!

C'est impossible! / Set-ahng-pawh-see-bl! — It's out of the question!

Tu n'est pas assez grand/e! (m/f) / Tew neh pah ah-say grawhng/d! — You're not old enough!

Pas de moyen! / Pah d'mwah-ehng! — No way!

Ça ne se fait pas. / Sah nuh suh feh pah. — That's not done.

Sois tranquille. (or) Ne t'inquiète pas. / Swah trawng-keel. (or) Nuh tahng-kee-eht pah. — Don't worry.

Ça s'arrangera. / Sah sah-rawnzh-rah. — It will turn out all right.

Ça pourrait arriver à n'importe qui. / Sah poor-ay ah-ree-vay ah nahng-pawhrt kee. — It could happen to anyone.

Ça va. Ça ne va pas. / Sah vah. Sah nuh vah pah. — It's all right. It's not right.

EXCLAMATIONS

Ça c'est gentil.　　　　　　　　　　That's nice.
Sah seh zhawng-tee.

Ça y est!　　　　　　　　　　　　　That's it!
Sah-ee-eh!

Ce n'est pas nécessaire.　　　　　　That's not necessary.
Suh neh pah nay-seh-sair.

Je m'en charge.　　　　　　　　　　I'll take care of it.
Zhuh mawng shahrzh.

Oop-la!　　　　　　　　　　　　　　Up you go!
Oop-lah!

Voilà du propre!　　　　　　　　　　What a mess!
Vwah-lah dew prawh-pr!

Quel dégoût!　　　　　　　　　　　Yuck!
Kell day-goo!

C'est vrai!　　　　　　　　　　　　　That's true!
Seh vreh!

Vraiment? Cela se peut!　　　　　　Is that so? That may be!
Vreh-mawng? Suh-lah suh puh!

Ce n'est pas ainsi.　　　　　　　　　That's not so.
Suh neh pah ahng-see.

Bien.... Voyons....　　　　　　　　　Well... Let's see...
B'yehng.... Vwah-yohng.....　　　　(An expression of hesitation
　　　　　　　　　　　　　　　　　　while considering a reply)

Eh bien!　　　　　　　　　　　　　　Well now!
Ay b'yehng!

Tiens! Pas possible!　　　　　　　　Indeed! You don't say!
T'yehng! Pah pawh-see-bl!

EXCLAMATIONS

Vraiment? Comment?	Really? What?
Vreh-mawng? Kawh-mawng?	
Comme d'habitude...	As usual . . .
Kawhm dah-bee-tewd	
Quel éternuement! A ta santé!	What a sneeze!
Kell ay-terr-newh-mawng! Ah tah sawng-tay!	God bless you!
Quel froncement!	What a frown!
Kell frawngs-mawng!	
Qu'est-ce qui ne va pas? De quoi s'agit-il?	What's wrong? What's up?
Kehs kee nuh vah pah? D'kwah sah-zhee-teel?	
Qu'est-ce que tu as?	What's the matter with you?
Kehs kuh tew ah?	
Pourquoi tu te plains?	Why are you complaining?
Poor-kwah tew tuh plahng?	
Cela est agaçant.	That's irritating.
Suh-lah eh-tah-gah-sawng.	
Je ne sais pas ce que ne va pas chez toi.	I don't know what's wrong with you.
Zhuh nuh say pah s'kuh nuh vah pah shay twah.	
J'ai presque autant de jouets que toi.	I have almost as many toys as you.
Zhay presk-oh-tawngt zhoo-eh kuh twah.	
C'est à prendre ou à laisser.	Take it or leave it.
Seht-ah prawng-dr oo ah leh-say.	
Va-t'en.	Get lost! (Slang)
Vah-tawng.	
Pourquoi pleures-tu?	Why are you crying?
Poor-kwah pluhr-tew?	
Regarde!	Look!
Ruh-gahrd!	

EXCLAMATIONS

Regarde-toi dans la glace.
Ruh-gahrd-twah dawng lah glahs.

Look at yourself in the mirror.

De grâce! Mon Dieu! Par exemple!
Duh grahs! Mohng d'yuh! Pahr eggs-awng-pl!

For goodness sake!

Que je suis bête!
Kuh zhuh swee beht!

How stupid of me!

Il n'y a pas de quoi rire!
Eel nee-yah pah d'kwah reer!

This is no laughing matter!

Tu mérites ça!
Tew may-reet sah!

It serves you right!

Tu ne devrais pas dire ça!
Tew nuh deh-vray pah deer sah!

You should not say that!

Je n'y peux rien.
Zhuh nee puh r'yehng.

I can't help it.

Je n'aime pas élever la voix!
Zhuh nehm pahs-ay-leh-vay lah vwah!

I don't like raising my voice!

Je suis fatigué/e d'attendre. (m/f)
Zhuh swee fah-tee-gay dah-tawng-dr.

I'm tired of waiting.

Je n'attendrai plus.
Zhuh nah-tawng-dr plewh.

I'll wait no longer.

J'en ai marre.
Zhawng ay mahr.

I'm fed up! I've had it!

A Dieu ne plaise!
Ah d'yuh nuh plehz!

God forbid!

Pour l'amour du ciel!
Poor lah-moor dew s'yehl!

Why on earth!

Mieux vaut santé que richesse. Health is better than wealth.

FÊTE d'ANNIVERSAIRE

Qu'est-ce que tu voudrais pour ton anniversaire?
Kehs kuh tew voo-dray poor tohng-nah-nee-vehr-sair?

Voudrais-tu avoir la boum:
Voo-dray-tew ah-vwahr lah boom:

  chez-nous,
  shay-noo,

  dans un restaurant,
  dawng-zuhng rehs-tawh-rawng,

  au parc,
  oh pahrk,

  ou à la plage?
  oo ah lah plazh?

BIRTHDAY PARTY

What would you like for your birthday?

Would you like to have the party:

  at home,

  in a restaurant,

  at the park,

  or at the beach?

BIRTHDAY PARTY

Nous inviterons tes amis.
Noo-zahng-vee-trohng tay-zah-mee.

We'll invite your friends.

Il y aura du gâteau, de la glace, des chapeaux,
des jeux et des cadeaux.
Eel ee awh-rah dew gah-toh, d'lah glahs,
day shah-poh, day zhuh ay day kah-doh.

We will have cake, ice cream,
  hats, games and presents.   *

Quel âge as-tu?
Kell ahzh ah-tew?

How old are you?

J'ai cinq ans.
Zhay sahngk awng.

I am five years old.

Je ne sais pas.
Zhuh nuh say pah.

I don't know.

Quand tu seras grand/e, qu'est-ce que
tu feras? (m/f)
Kawng tew seh-rah grawng/d, kehs kuh tew
feh-rah?

When you are grown up,
what you will be?

Fais un voeux.
Feh-zuhng vuh.

Make a wish.

Souffle les bougies.
Soo-fl lay boo-zhee.

Blow out the candles.

Coupe le gâteau.
Koop luh gah-toh.

Cut the cake.   *

Divise le gâteau en huit morceaux.
Dee-veez luh gah-toh awng weet mawhr-soh.

Divide the cake into eight
pieces.

Quel beau cadeau j'ai reçu.
Kell boh kah-doh zhay reh-sewh.

What a beautiful present
I've received.

Quelle bonne boum.
Kell buhn boom.

What a nice party.

Les jours se suivent et ne se ressemblent pas. Tomorrow is another day.

L'HEURE *du* COUCHER   BEDTIME

This is a fine time to read a story or book in French to your child. The language he hears before going to sleep will linger in his mind during the night. This might also be a golden opportunity to learn and recite prayers in French.

Quel bâillement! Tu bâilles.	What a yawn!
Kell bigh-yuh-mawng! Tew bigh-yuh	You're yawning.
Es-tu fatigué/e? (m/f)	Are you tired?
Eh-tew fah-tee-gay?	
As-tu sommeil?	Are you sleepy?
Ah-tew sawh-may?	
C'est l'heure du coucher.	It's time for bed.
Seh luhr dew koo-shay.	
Je te mets au lit.	I'm putting you to bed.
Zhuh tuh meh oh lee.	
Veux-tu que je te mette au lit?	Do you want me to put you to bed?
Vuh-tew kuh zhuh tuh mett oh lee?	

BEDTIME

Va chercher ton livre. Je te lirai un conte
avant de te coucher.
Vah shehr-shay tohng lee-vr. Zhuh tuh lee-ray
uhng kawngt ah-vawng d'tuh koo-shay.

Go get your book. I'll read
you a story before you go
to bed.

Monte te coucher.
Mawngt tuh koo-shay.

Go upstairs to bed.

As-tu la permission de regarder la télévision?
Ah-tew lah pehr-mee-s'yohng d'ruh-gahr-day
lah tay-lay-v'z'yohng?

Do you have permission
to watch television?

Déshabille-toi.
Day-zah-bee-twah.

Take off your clothes.

Mets le pyjama.
Meh luh pee-zhah-mah.

Put on your pajamas. *

Pends ta chemise sur le cintre.
Pawng tah shuh-meez sewr luh sahng-tr.

Hang your shirt on the
hanger.

Range tous tes vêtements.
Rawngzh too tay veht-mawng.

Put all your clothes away.

Ces chaussettes ont besoin d'être lavées.
Say shoh-sett ohng buh-zwahng deh-tr lah-vay.

These socks need *
laundering.

Es-tu prêt/e à te coucher? (m/f)
Eh-tew preh/ t ah tuh koo-shay?

Are you ready for bed?

Je suis (presque) prêt/e. (m/f)
Zhuh swee (prehsk) preh/t.

I'm (almost) ready.

Dis <<Bonne nuit >> à papa.
Dee <<buhn nwee >> ah pah-pah.

Say, "Goodnight" to
daddy.

As-tu fait tes prières?
Ah-tew feh tay pree-y'air?

Did you say your prayers?

112

BEDTIME

Tu deviens lourd/e. (m/f) Tew duh-v'yehng loor/d.	You're getting heavy.
Ferme les yeux. Fehrm lay-zyuh.	Close your eyes.
J'ai quelque chose dans l'oeil. Zhay kell-kuh shohz dawng loy-yuh.	I have something in my eye.
Sois tranquille. Tais-toi. Swah trawng-keel. Teh-twah.	Be still. Be quiet.
Fais de beaux rêves. Feh d'boh rehv.	Pleasant dreams.
Endors-toi. Tu dois dormir. Awng-dawhr-twah. Tew dwah dawhr-meer.	Go to sleep. You have to sleep.
Est-ce que tu es bien? Ehs kuh tew eh b'yehng?	Are you comfortable?
Tu n'es pas encore au lit? Tew neh pah-zawng-kawhr oh lee?	You're not in bed yet?
Recouche-toi. Ruh-koosh-twah.	Go back to bed.
Il n'est pas trop tôt pour aller se coucher. Eel neh pah troh toh poor ah-lay suh koo-shay.	It's not too early to go to bed.
Veux-tu la lumière allumée? Vuh-tew lah lewh-m'yair ah-lewh-may?	Do you want the light lit?
/Je/ Maman/ Papa/ t'aime. /Zhuh/ Mah-mawng/ Pah-pah/ tehm.	/I/ Mommy/ Daddy/ love(s) you.
Embrasse-moi. Awng-brass-mwah.	Give me a kiss.

BEDTIME

Que Dieu te bénisse. Kuh d'yuh tuh bay-nees.	God bless you.
Tu es réveillé/e? endormi/e? (m/f) Tew eh ray-veh-yay? awng-dawhr-mee?	Are you awake? asleep?
Tu as la bougeotte. Tew ah lah boozh-awht.	You're fidgety.
Es-tu malade? mouillé/e? (m/f) Eh-tew mah-lahd? moo-yay?	Are you sick? wet?
/Elle/Il/ dort. Ne/ la/ le/ réveille pas. /Ell/ Eel/ dawhr. Nuh/ lah/ luh/ ray-vay pah.	/She/ He/ is sleeping. Don't wake /her/ him/.
Pourquoi ne dors-tu pas (encore)? Poor-kwah nuh dawhr-tew pah (zawng-kawhr)?	Why are you not (yet) asleep?
As-tu du mal à t'endormir? Ah-tew dew mahl ah tawng-dawhr-meer?	Are you having a hard time falling asleep?
Je ne peux pas m'endormir avec ce bruit! Zhuh nuh puh pah mawng-dohr-meer ah-vehk suh brwee!	I can't go to sleep with that noise!
Que désires-tu, /mon petit/ ma petite/? (m/f) Kuh day-zeer-tew, /mohng p'tee/ mah p'teet/?	What do you want, my little one?
Tu t'es gratté/e le visage pendant le sommeil. (m/f) Tew teh grah-tay luh vee-zahzh pawng-dawng luh soh-may.	You scratched your face in your sleep.
Tu ne te sens pas bien? Tew nuh tuh sawng pah b'yehng?	Don't you feel well?
As-tu le vertige? Tu as de la fièvre. Ah-tew luh vehr-teezh? Tew ah d'lah fee-eh-vr.	Are you dizzy? You have a fever.
Tes glandes sont gonflées. Tay glawnd sohng gawng-flay.	Your glands are swollen.

BEDTIME

Tu as des boutons sur ta poitrine. (La varicelle)
Tew ah day boo-tohng sewr tah pwah-treen.
(Lah vah-ree-sell)

There are spots on your
chest. (chicken pox)

Montre ta langue.
Mawng-tr tah lawng.

Stick out your tongue.

Tu as un rhume. Tu tousses.
Tew ah uhng rewhm. Tew tooss.

You have a cold.
You're coughing.

Tu auras besoin de quelque chose contre
cette toux.
Tew awh-rah buh-zwahng d'kell-kuh shohz
kawng-tr sett too.

You'll need something for
that cough.

Prends ce médicament. Ouvre la bouche.
Prawng suh may-dee-kah-mawng. Oo-vr lah
boosh.

Take this medicine.
Open your mouth.

(Demain) tu dois rester au lit.
(Duh-mahng) tew dwah reh-stay oh lee.

(Tomorrow) you'll have
to stay in bed.

As-tu mal /au bras/ au pied/?
Ah-tew mahl /oh brah/ oh p'yay/?

Does your /arm/ foot/ hurt?

Quel/ pied/ dent/ te fait mal?
Kell/ p'yay/ dawng/ tuh feh mahl?

Which/ foot/ tooth/ hurts?

Veux-tu un nouveau pansement pour le doigt?
Vuh-tew uhng noo-voh pawngs-mohng poor
luh dwah?

Do you want a new bandaid
for your finger?   *

Voilà. Ça va mieux?
Vwah-lah. Sah vah m'yewh?

There. All better?

As-tu bien dormi?
Ah-tew b'yehng dawhr-mee?

Did you sleep well?

Dors bien. Fais dodo.
Dohr b'yehng. Feh doh-doh.

Sleep well. Go sleepy byes.

Noël au balcon, Pâques aux tisons. A warm Christmas spells a cold Easter.

Le TEMPS   WEATHER

"Everybody talks about it." So the saying goes. Now you and your child can talk about it in French! Try sharing a picture book on weather with your child and discuss the pictures using French. This could be more of a "school" kind of chapter if you and your child want to play school. Flash cards to make, maps to draw, temperatures to record, fun to be had!

Il fait jour. Eel feh zhoor.	It's light.
Quelle belle journée. Kell bell zhoor-nay.	What a beautiful day.
Il fait du soleil. Eel feh dew soh-lay-yuh.	It's sunny.
Il n'y a pas de nuages. Eel nee ah pah d'noo-ahzh.	There are no clouds.
Il fait beau. Eel feh boh.	The sun is shining.
Il fait/ très chaud/ chaud/ aujourd'hui. Eel feh/ treh shoh/ shoh/ oh-zhoor-dwee.	It's/ hot/ warm/ today.

WEATHER

Il fait terriblement chaud. C'est l'été.
Eel feh tuh-ree-bl-mawng shoh. Seh lay-tay.

It's terribly hot. It's summer.*

Nous sommes en pleine canicule.
Noo sawhm awng plehn kah-nee-kool.

We're having a heat wave.

Il n'y a aucun souffle de vent.
Eel nee-yah oh-kuhng soo-fl d'vawng.

There's not a breath of wind.

Il fait du vent.
Eel feh dew vawng.

It's windy.

Quelle belle nuit.
Kell bell nwee.

What a beautiful night.

Il fait (assez) /frais/ froid/.
Eel feh (ah-say) /freh/ frwah/.

It's (rather) / cool/ cold/.

Le temps se refroidit.
Luh tawng suh ruh-frwah-dee.

The weather is cooling down.

Tu as besoin d'un / manteau/ pull/.
Tew ah buh-zwahng duhng /mawng-toh/ puhl/.

You need a / coat/ pullover/.

Le temps est couvert.
Luh tawng eh koo-vehr.

It's cloudy.

Le ciel est couvert
Luh s'yehl eh koo-vehr.

The sky is overcast.

Il pleut (à sceau).
Eel pluh (ah so).

It's raining (buckets).

Il pleut à verse.
Eel pluh ah vehrs.

It's pouring.

Les gouttes de pluie tombent.
Lay goot d'plwee tawng-buh.

Raindrops are falling.

117

WEATHER

Regarde la pluie.
Ruh-gahrd lah plwee.

Look at the rain.

J'aime beaucoup me promener sous la pluie.
Zhem boh-koo muh prawh-m'nay soo
lah plwee.

I love to walk in the rain.

La rue est pleine de flaques.
Lah rew eh plehn d'flahk.

The street is full of puddles.*

Il mouille.
Eel moo-ee-yuh.

It's wet (outside).

Ote tes souliers.
Oht tay soo-lyay.

Take off your shoes.

Tes pieds sont mouillés.
Tay p'yay sohng moo-yay.

Your feet are wet.

Quelle mauvaise journée!
Kell moh-vay-zhoor-nay!

What an unpleasant day!

Quel temps affreux!
Kell tawng-zaf-ruh!

What awful weather!

Quel vilain temps!
Kell vee-lahng tawng!

What nasty weather!

Il fait mauvais.
Eel feh moh-veh.

The weather is bad.

Il devient sombre.
Eel duh-v'yehng sawng-br.

It's getting dark.

Le ciel est /sombre/gris/.
Luh s'yehl eh /sawng-br/ gree/.

The sky is / dark/ gray/.

Il fera bientôt nuit.
Eel feh-rah b'yehng-toh nwee.

It will be dark soon.

WEATHER

Il y a du tonnerre et des éclairs.
Eel ee ah dew tohng-nair ay day-zay-klair.

There's thunder and lightning. *

Quelle tempête!
Kell tawng-pet!

What a storm!

Quel orage!
Kell oh-rahzh!

What a storm!

Quel brouillard!
Kell broo-yahr!

What fog!

Attends que la pluie s'arrête.
Ah-tawng kuh lah plwee sah-reht.

Wait until the rain stops.

Vois l'arc-en-ciel.
Vwah lahrk-awng-s'yehl.

See the rainbow.

C'est un vrai jour d'hiver.
Seh-tuhng vray zhoor dee-vair.

It's a real winter day.

Il gèle dehors.
Eel zhehl deh-ohr.

It's freezing outside.

La neige commence à tomber.
Lah nehzh kawh-mawngs ah tawng-bay.

It's beginning to snow.

Il neige.
Eel nehzh.

It's snowing.

Il neige depuis trois jours.
Eel nehzh duh-pwee twah zhoor.

It's been snowing for three days.

Les flocons de neige tombent.
Lay floh-kohng d'nehzh tawng-buh.

Snowflakes are falling.

Regarde la neige.
Ruh-gahrd lah nehzh.

Look at the snow.

WEATHER

Allons jouer dans la neige.
Ah-lohng zhoo-ay dawng lah nehzh.

Tirons nos luges.
Tee-rohng noh lewzh.

Glissons sur la colline.
Glee-sohng sewr lah kawh-leen.

Comme la neige étincèle!
Kawhm lah nehzh ay-tahng-sehl!

Peut-être nous pouvons bâtir un bonhomme de neige?
Puh-teh-tr noo poo-vohng bah-teer uhng buhn-num d'nehzh?

/La neige/ La pluie/s'est arrêtée.
/Lah nehzh/ Lah plwee/ seh-tah-reh-tay.

La neige fond.
Lah nehzh fohng.

Pluie, pluie va-t-en. Reviens un autre jour!
Plwee, plwee vah-tawng. Ruh-v'yehng uhng oh-tr zhoor!

Let's go play in the snow.

Let's get our sleds.

Let's slide down the hill.

How the snow sparkles!

Perhaps we can build a snowman?

/The snow/ rain/ has stopped.

The snow is melting.

Rain, rain go away.
Come again another day!

Il y a un temps pour tout. There is a time for everything.

L'HEURE   TIME

Il est une heure.
Eel eht ewn uhr.

It's one o'clock.

Il est deux heures.
Eel eh duh-zuhr.

It's two o'clock.

Il est trois heures quinze.
Eel eh trwah-zuhr kahngz.

It's three fifteen.

Il est quatre heures et demi.
Eel eh kahtr-uhr ay d'mee.

It's four thirty.

Il est cinq heures moins le quart.
Eel eh sahngk-uhr mwahng luh kahr.

It's four forty-five.

Il est six heures vingt.
Eel eh see-zuhr vahng.

It's six twenty.

Il est sept heures moins vingt.
Eel eh set-uhr mwahng vahng.

It's six forty.

TIME

Il est huit heures.
Eel eh weet-uhr.

It's eight o'clock.

Il est neuf heures.
Eel eh nuv-uhr.

It's nine o'clock.

Il est dix heures.
Eel eh dee-zuhr.

It's ten o'clock.

Il est onze heures.
Eel eht-ohng-zuhr.

It's eleven o'clock.

Il est /minuit/ midi/.
Eel eh /mee-nwee/mee-dee/.

It's /midnight/ noon/.

C'est/ le matin/ l'après-midi/.
Seh/ luh mah-tahng/ lah-preh-mee-dee/.

It's /morning/afternoon/.

Il fait nuit.
Eel feh nwee.

It's night.

Il est/ tôt/ tard/.
Eel eh/ toh/ tahr/.

It's/ early/ late/.

Aussitôt que possible.
Oh-see-toh kuh poh-see-bl.

As soon as possible.

Juste à ce moment...
Zhewst ah suh moh-mawng...

Just then...

A partir de maintenant...
Ah pah-teer d'mahng-t'nawng...

From now on...

Le temps fuit!
Luh tawng fwee!

Time flies!

Il était une fois...
Eel ay-tay ewn fwah...

Once upon a time...

Faute de grives, on mange des merles. Half a loaf is better than none.

QUANTITÉS

Quel âge as-tu?
Kell ahzh ah-tew?

Quel âge a/maman/ papa/?
Kell ahzh ah/ mah-mawng/ pah-pah/?

Combien de doigts vois-tu?
Kohng-b'yehng d'dwah vwah-tew?

Combien y-en-a-t'il?
Kohng b'yehng ee-yawng-nah-teel?

En voilà seulement un.
Awng vwah-lah suhl-mawng uhng.

En voilà seulement quatre.
Awng vwah-lah suhl-mawng kah-tr.

Je n'en ai pas.
Zhuh nawng-nay pah.

QUANTITIES

How old are you?

How old is/ mommy/ daddy/?

How many fingers do you see?

How many are there?

There is only one. (of them)

There are only four. (of them)

I have none. (of them)

QUANTITIES

Il n'y en a aucun.
Eel nee-awng ah oh-kuhng.

There are none. (of them)

Mets chacun à sa place exacte.
Meh shah-kuhng ah sah plahs eggs-akt.

Put each one in the right place.

Tous les gâteaux secs sont mangés.
Too lay gah-toh sehk sohng mawng-zhay.

All the cookies have been eaten.

Après quinze vient seize.
Ah-preh kahngz v'yehng sehz.

After fifteen comes sixteen.

Compte de trois à dix.
Kawngt d'trwah ah dees.

Count from three to ten.

Compte jusqu'à vingt.
Kawngt zhews-kah vahng.

Count (up) to twenty.

Un et un font deux.
Uhng ay uhng fohng duh.

One and one make two.

Quatre moins deux font deux.
Kahtr mwahng duh fohng duh.

Four minus two make two.

Deux fois un font deux.
Duh fwah uhng fohng duh.

Two times one make two.

Deux, quatre, six sont des nombres pairs.
Duh, kahtr, seess sohng day nohng-br pehr.

Two, four, six are even numbers.

Trois, cinq, sept sont des nombres impairs.
Trwah, sahngk, seht sohng day nohng-br ahng-pehr.

Three, five, seven are odd numbers.

Ton chiffre huit ressemble à un trois.
Tohng shee-fr weet reh-sawng-bl ah uhng twah.

Your figure eight looks like a three.

deux moitiés
duh mwah-tee-yay

two halves

QUANTITIES

une moitié, un tiers, un quart ewn mwah-tee-yay, uhng t'yair, uhng kahr	one half, one third, one fourth
un peu / moins/ plus/ uhng puh /mwahng/ plewh (or plewhs)/	a little/ less/ more
quelques kell-kuh	some, a few
plusieurs plewh-zyuhr	several
et puis encore? ay pwee awng-kohr?	and then what else?
Cela (Ça) suffit. (or) C'est assez. Suh-lah (Sah) soo-fee. (or) Seht-ah-say.	That's enough.

Bâtir des châteaux en Espagne. To build castles in the air.

L'ALPHABET   ALPHABET

A	B	C	D	E	F	G	H	I
Ah	bay	say	day	uh	eff	zhay	ahsh	ee

J	K	L	M	N	O	P	Q	R
zhee	kah	ell	em	en	oh	pay	kew	air

S	T	U	V	W	X	Y	Z
ess	tay	ew	vay	doo-bluh-vay	eeks	ee-grek	zed

Quelle lettre est-ce?   What letter is this?
Kell leh-tr ess?

Voici la lettre A.   Here is the letter A.
Vwah-see lah leh-tr ah.

Quelle est cette lettre?   What is this letter?
Kell eh sett leh-tr?

Lis cette lettre.   Read this letter.
Lee sett leh-tr.

ALPHABET

Combien de lettres y a-t-il dans le mot chat?
Kawng-b'yehng d'leh-tr ee-yah-teel dawng luh moh shah?

How many letters are there in the word cat?

Où est la lettre H?
Oo eh lah leh-tr ahsh ?

Where is the letter H?

Montre du doigt la lettre J.
Mawng-tr dew dwah lah leh-tr zhee.

Point to the letter J.

Que veut dire ce mot?
Kuh vuh deer suh moh?

What does this word mean?

Veux-tu répéter ce mot?
Vuh-tew ray-pay-tay suh moh?

Will you repeat this word?

A qui est ce nom?
Ah kee eh suh nohng?

Whose name is this?

Ne tiens pas ton crayon si fortement.
Nuh t'yehng pah tohng kray-yohng see fawhrt-uh-mawng.

Don't hold your pencil so tightly.

Je ne peux pas lire l'écriture.
Zhuh nuh puh pah leer lay-kree-tewhr.

I can't read the writing.

Tiens-le comme ça.
T'yehng-luh kawhm sah.

Hold it like this.

Pour le L écris vers le bas, puis à droite.
Poor luh ell ay-kree vehr luh bah, pwee ah drwaht.

Write down and over for L.

La vieille Mère Oie   Old Mother Goose

Les COMPTINES   NURSERY RHYMES

Nursery rhymes are a marvelous way to soothe a crying baby, fill a few empty minutes, or just enjoy for their own rhythm. Trusting that the reader already knows the English version of these rhymes, we have chosen to translate them more closely to the French text so that, even though stilted at times, the literal translation of the French words will be understood by the reader.

Agneau blanc	Baa Baa Black Sheep
Agneau blanc	White sheep,
as-tu un peu de laine?	have you a little wool?
Oui monsieur, oui monsieur, trois sacs pleins.	Yes sir, yes sir, three bags full.
Un pour mon maître,	One for my master,
L'autre pour madame,	the other for the dame,
Un pour le garçon	One for the boy
qui vit un peu plus loin.	who lives a little further.
Humpti-Dumpti	Humpty Dumpty
Humpti-Dumpti à cheval sur un mur;	Humpty Dumpty astride a wall;
Humpti-Dumpti fit une chute dure;	Humpty Dumpty had a great fall.
Tous les destriers, les hallebardiers	All the battle horses, the king's men
N'arrivaient pas à le rafistoler.	Couldn't put Humpty Dumpty together again.

Three Little Kittens

Three little kittens their mittens
they lost; they whimpered:
Oh, mother dear, as we fear,
we have lost our mittens.

Your gloves? Naughty kittens!
You will have no doughnuts!
Meow, meow, meow, meow,
No, you will have no doughnuts.

The three little kittens their mittens
they have found; they cried:
Oh, mother dear, see here, see here,
we have found our mittens!

Good, put them on, my silly kittens,
and eat your doughnuts.
Purr, purr, purr, purr,
Oh give us our doughnuts.

Three Blind Mice

Three blind mice,
see how they run!
They were running after the farmer's wife,
who cuts their tail
waving a cleaver;
Have you ever seen such a scuffle
As three blind mice?

Jack and Jill

Jack and Jill on the mountain
For a pail of sweet water they were looking;
Jack fell and broke his head,
Jill tumbled behind.

Jack jumped up and saved himself,
His sorrow was bitter;
He went to bed, and bandaged his head
With vinegar paper.

Les trois minets

Les trois minets leurs gantelets
Perdirent; ils pleurnichaient:
Oh, chère Maman, comme nous craignons
D'avoir perdu nos gants.

Vos gantelets? Méchants minets!
Vous n'aurez pas de beignets!
Miaou, miaou, miaou, miaou,
Non, vous n'aurez pas de beignets.

Les trois minets leurs gantelets
Trouvèrent; ils s'écriaient:
Oh, chère Maman, dis-donc, dis-donc,
Nous avons trouvé nos gants!

Bon, mettez-les, mes sots minets,
Et mangez vos beignets.
Ron-ron, ron-ron, ron-ron, ron-ron,
O donne-nous nos beignets.

Trois souris aveugles

Trois souris aveugles,
vois comme elles courent!
Elles couraient après la femme du fermier,
Qui leur coupa la queue
brandissant un couperet;
As-tu jamais vu une telle mêlée
Que trois souris aveugles?

Jean et Jeanne

Jean et Jeanne sur la montagne
Un seau d'eau douce cherchèrent;
Jean tomba, la tête se cassa,
Jeanne culbuta derrière.

Jean sursauta et se sauva,
Sa douleur était aigre;
Il s'alita, et la tête se banda
En papier kraft au vinaigre.

Ce petit porc

Ce petit porc s'en fut au marché,
Ce petit porc ne bougea point,
Ce petit porc mangea du rosbif,
Ce petit porc n'eut rien de rien.
Ce petit porc cria Ki! Ki! Ki! Ki!
Tout le long du chemin.

Mademoiselle Mouffue

Mademoiselle Mouffue,
Sur l'herbe touffue,
Goûtait son café au lait.
Une affreuse araignée,
Survenant à côté,
L'a rudement épouvantée.

Au lit, au lit!

"Au lit, au lit!" crie l'Endormi;
"Attends un peu," dit la Lente;
"Un bout de pain," fit Crève-la-Faim,
"Et puis après on monte."

La Noël arrive bientôt

La Noël arrive bientôt;
Les oies sont grasses à lard;
Prière de mettre deux sous
Dans le chapeau du vieillard.
Si vous n'avez pas deux sous,
Un centime suffira.
Si vous n'avez pas de centime,
Le Bon Dieu vous bénira.

This Little Piggy

This little piggy went to market,
This little piggy didn't stir at all,
This little piggy ate roast beef,
This little piggy had absolutely nothing.
This little piggy cried wee!wee!wee!
All the way.

Little Miss Muffet

Little Miss Muffet
Sat on thick grass,
Tasting her coffee with milk.
A frightful spider,
Happened beside her,
And rudely scared her.

To Bed, to Bed!

"To bed, to bed," cried sleepyhead;
"Wait awhile," said slowpoke;
"An end of bread," said the starveling,
"And then we'll go up (to bed)."

Christmas Is Coming

Christmas is coming soon;
The geese are getting fat.
Please put two pennies
In the old man's hat.
If you haven't got two pennies,
A half-penny will do.
If you haven't got a half-penny,
May God bless you.

Prayers	*Les Prières*
Our Father	*Notre Père*
Our Father, who art in heaven, hallowed be thy name; Thy kingdom come, Thy will be done on earth as it is in heaven. Give us today our bread; and forgive us our offenses as we forgive also those who have offended us. And lead us not into temptation, but deliver us from evil. Amen.	Notre Père, qui es aux cieux, que ton nom soit sanctifié, que ton règne vienne, que ta volonté soit faite sur la terre comme au ciel. Donne-nous aujourd'hui notre pain de ce jour. Pardonne-nous nos offenses comme nous pardonnons aussi à ceux qui nous ont offensés. Et ne nous soumets pas à la tentation, mais délivre-nous du Mal. Amen.
Psalm 23	*Le berger d' Israël*
The Lord is my shepherd, there is nothing I shall want. He leads me near green pastures, near calm waters he leads me. He comforts my soul. He guides me by the right path, for the honor of his name. If I cross a dark valley, I fear nothing; You are near me. Your rod and staff reassure me. Before me you prepare a table in the sight of my foes; You annoint my head with oil; my cup overflows. Thus goodness and kindness accompany me all the days of my life; I will live in the house of the Lord forever.	Le Seigneur est mon berger, Je ne manquerai de rien. Il me mène en des prés verdoyants, près des eaux calmes il me conduit. Il réconforte mon âme, il me guide par le droit chemin, pour l'honneur de son nom. Si je traverse une vallée obscure, je ne crains rien : tu es près de moi; ta houlette et ton bâton me rassurent. Devant moi tu dresses une table, face à mes adversaires; Tu verses le parfum sur ma tête, ma coupe est débordante. Ainsi grâce et bonheur m'accompagnent, tous les jours de ma vie; J'habiterai la maison du Seigneur, dans la suite des jours.
Prayer before Meals	*Avant de Repas*
Bless us O Lord and these Thy gifts which we are about to receive. Amen.	Benissez-nous mon Dieu ainsi que la nourriture que nous allons prendre. Amen.

VOCABULARY

VOCABULARY

Famille — The Family and Other Persons

maman/ mère	mommy/ mother	le petit-fils	grandson
papa/ père	daddy/ father	la fille	daughter
grand-mère	grandmother	le fils	son
grand-père	grandfather	la soeur	sister
grand-maman	grandma	le frère	brother
grand-papa	grandpa	la femme	woman
la tante	aunt	l'homme	man
l'oncle	uncle	la jeune fille	girl
la cousine (f)	cousin	le garçon	boy
le cousin (m)	cousin	les enfants	children
la nièce	niece	Monsieur	Mister
le neveu	nephew	Madame	Missus
la petite-fille	grand-daughter	Mademoiselle	Miss

Noms d'affection — Endearments

mon bébé	my baby	chouchou	my dear
ma poupée	my doll	poulette	sweetheart
ma princesse	my princess	mon petit	my little one
mon prince	my prince	ma petite	my little one
mon trésor	my treasure	mon petit chou	honey, sweetie
chéri/e (m/f)	sweetheart	mon petit poussin	my little chick

Couleurs — Colors

vert/e	green	jaune	yellow
bleu/e	blue	violet/te	violet
noir/e	black	rose	pink
blanc/he	white	brun/e	brown
orange	orange	gris/e	gray
rouge	red	beige	beige

Jours de la semaine — Days of the Week

lundi	Monday	vendredi	Friday
mardi	Tuesday	samedi	Saturday
mercredi	Wednesday	dimanche	Sunday
jeudi	Thursday		

VOCABULARY

Mois de l'année   Months of the Year

janvier	January	juillet	July
février	February	août	August
mars	March	septembre	September
avril	April	octobre	October
mai	May	novembre	November
juin	June	décembre	December

Saisons de l'année   Seasons of the Year

le printemps	spring	l'autommne (m or f)	autumn
l'été	summer (m)	l'hiver (m)	winter

Fêtes de l'année   Holidays of the Year

l'anniversaire	birthday	Le Jour de la découverte de l'Amérique	October 12th
Le Nouvel An	New Year's Day		
La (Fête) St Valentin	St. Valentine's Day		
La (Fête) St Patrick	St. Patrick's Day	La Veille de la Toussaint	Halloween
La Pâque	Passover		
Pâques	Easter	Le Jour des actions de grâce	Thanksgiving
La Fête des Mères	Mother's Day		
La Fête des Pères	Father's Day	La (Fête) Noël	Christmas
Le Jour de l'indépendance	July 4th	La Veille de Noël	Christmas Eve

Chambre d'enfants   Nursery

la baignoire	bath tub	la veilleuse	night light
le livre	book	la tétine	pacifier
la poussette	carriage	la couche à jeter	pamper
le berceau	crib	le tableau	picture
la couche	diaper	le parc	play pen
le biberon	feeding bottle	la chaise à bascule	rocker
la chaise haute	high chair	l'épingle de sûreté	safety pin
La Mère d'Oie	Mother Goose	la poussette	stroller
		le joujou	toy

VOCABULARY

Joujoux		Toys	
la balle	ball	le pinceau	paint brush
le ballon	balloon	la colle	paste
la batte	bat	le livre d'images	picture book
la perle	bead	la tirelire	piggy bank
la bicyclette, le vélo	bicycle	l'avion (à réaction)	plane (jet)
		la marionnette	puppet
le cube	block	le casse-tête	puzzle
le bateau (à voile)	boat (sail)	la voiture de course	race car
le bull-dozer	bull dozer	le râteau	rake
l'autobus	bus	le hochet	rattle
l'auto, la voiture	car	la bague	ring
l'échiquier (m)	chess board	la fusée	rocket
la pâte à modeler	clay	le cheval à bascule	rocking horse
le clown	clown	la corde	rope
le cowboy	cowboy	le bac à sable	sandbox
le pastel	crayon	les ciseaux (m)	scissors
la poupée	doll	la trottinette	scooter
la maison de poupée	doll house	la balance	seesaw
		la pelle	shovel
le tambour	drum	le patin (à glace)	skate (ice)
la boucle d'oreille	earring	le patin à roulettes	skate (roller)
la canne à pêche	fishing rod	la planche à roulettes	skateboard
le fort	fort	le traîneau	sled
le jeu	game	le toboggan	slide
la mappemonde	globe	le soldat (de plomb)	soldier (lead)
l'hélicoptère	helicopter		
le cerceau	hoop	le soldat (de bois)	soldier (wooden)
la trompette	horn	le sous-marin	submarine
l'Indien	Indian	la balançoire	swing
la boîte à surprise	jack-in-the box	le tank	tank (military)
la corde à sauter	jump rope	le service à thé	tea service
le cerf-volant	kite	l'ours en peluche (m)	teddy bear
la bille	marble		
le masque	mask	la raquette de tennis	tennis racquet
le collier	necklace		
la boîte de peinture	paint box	la tente	tent

VOCABULARY

la toupie	top	le camion citerne	oil truck
la boîte à joujoux	toy box	la voiture de dépannage	tow truck
le tracteur	tractor		
le train (électrique)	train (electric)		
le tricycle	tricycle	le camion-jouet	wagon
le camion	truck	la brouette	wheelbarrow
le camion-benne	dump truck	le sifflet	whistle
la voiture des pompiers	fire truck	le xylophone	xylophone
le camion à ordures	garbage truck		

Vêtements — Clothes

le sac à dos	backpack	le caoutchouc	rubber
la robe de chambre	bathrobe	la sandale	sandal
le maillot de bain	bathing suit	l'écharpe	scarf
la ceinture	belt	la chemise	shirt
le bavoir	bib	le soulier	shoe
le chemisier	blouse	le lacet	shoe lace
la botte	boot	les shorts	shorts
la casquette	cap	la jupe	skirt
le veston	coat	le jupon	slip
la robe	dress	la pantoufle	slipper
le gant	glove	la chaussure de gym	sneaker
le mouchoir	handkerchief		
le chapeau	hat	le costume de ski	snow suit
le talon haut	high heel (pump)	la chaussette	sock
la jaquette	jacket	le bas	stocking
les jeans	jeans	le tee-shirt	tee-shirt
la moufle	mitten	la cravate	tie
la chemise de nuit	nightgown	les collants	tights/pantyhose
la salopette	overalls	le parapluie	umbrella
le manteau, le pardessus	overcoat	les caleçons	underpants (boys)
le pyjama	pajamas	la chemise de dessous	undershirt
le slip	panties		
le pantalon	slacks	les sous-vêtements	underwear
le sac à main	pocketbook	le portefeuille	wallet
l'imperméable (m)	rain coat	le blouson	windbreaker

VOCABULARY

Divertissements / Entertainments

le parc des attractions	amusement park	le parc	park
l'aquarium (m)	aquarium	la boum	party
la plage	beach	le pique-nique	picnic
le badminton	badminton	le parc de jeux	playground
le baseball	baseball	la lecture	reading
le basketball	basketball	la récréation	recess (school)
le jeu de boules	bowling	le restaurant	restaurant
le camping	camping	l'aviron	rowing
le cirque	circus	faire de la voile	sailing
le concert	concert	faire des achats	shopping
le cyclisme	cycling	le patinage	skating
la fête foraine	fair	le football	soccer
la pêche	fishing	les jeux	sports
le football américain	football	faire la collection de timbres	stamp collecting
le jeu	game, match	la natation	swimming
le golf	golf	le tennis	tennis
la gymnastique	gymnastics	le volleyball	volleyball
le hiking	hiking	la marche	walking
le film	movie	la planche à voile	windsurfing
le cinéma	movie theatre	le jardin zoologique	zoo
le musée	museum		

Corps humain / Human Body

la cheville	ankle	les yeux	eyes
le bras	arm	le visage, la figure	face
le dos	back	le doigt	finger
le ventre	belly	l'ongle	fingernail
le nombril	belly button	le front	forehead
la joue	cheek	les cheveux (m)	hair
la poitrine	chest	la main	hand
le menton	chin	la tête	head
l'oreille (m)	ear	le talon	heel
le coude	elbow	la hanche	hip
l'oeil (m)	eye	la mâchoire	jaw
le sourcil	eyebrow	le genou	knee
la paupière	eyelid	la jambe	leg

137

VOCABULARY

la lèvre	lip	la gorge	throat
la bouche	mouth	l'orteil (m)	toe
le cou	neck	la langue	tongue
le nez	nose	la dent	tooth
l'épaule (f)	shoulder	la taille	waist
l'estomac (m)	stomach	le poignet	wrist
le pouce	thumb		

Boissons / Beverages

la bière	beer	le jus d'orange	orange juice
le chocolat (chaud)	cocoa (warm)	l'orangeade (m)	orangeade
le café (au lait)	coffee (with milk)	le soda	soda
la limonade	lemon soda	(la tasse de) thé	(cup of) tea
le citronnade	lemonade	le thé au citron	tea with lemon
le lait	milk	l'eau (glacée)	water (iced)
		le vin	wine

Récipients / Containers

le sac	bag	le bocal	jar
la bouteille	bottle	le couvercle	top, cover
la boîte	box, can	le tube	tube
le carton	carton	le papier	wrapper
la caisse	crate	d'emballage	
l'enveloppe (f)	envelope		

Desserts / Desserts

la tarte aux pommes	apple pie	le beignet	doughnut
		le blanc-manger	gelatin
le gâteau (au chocolat)	cake (chocolate)	la glace	ice cream
		le milk-shake	milk shake
les bonbons	candy	la crêpe	pancake
le gâteau sec	cookie	la pâtisserie	pastry
le croissant	crescent	le quatre-quart	pound cake
le flan	custard	le pudding	pudding
la crème	custard	le riz au lait	rice pudding
la crème au caramel	custard (caramel)	le yaourt	yoghurt
la crème à la vanille	custard (vanilla)		

VOCABULARY

Légumes — Vegetables

l'asperge (f)	asparagus	l'oignon (m)	onion
la betterave	beet	le persil	parsley
le chou de Bruxelles	Brussel sprout	le petit pois	pea
		le poivron	pepper
le chou	cabbage	la pomme de terre	potato
la carotte	carrot	la citrouille	pumpkin
le chou-fleur	cauliflower	le radis	radish
le céleri	celery	les épinards	spinach
un épi de maïs	(ear of) corn	le haricot vert	stringbean
le concombre	cucumber	la tomate	tomato
l'ail (m)	garlic	le navet	turnip
la laitue	lettuce		
le champignon	mushroom		

Viande — Meat

le lard	bacon	la côtelette, de mouton	lamb chop
le poulet (rôti)	chicken (roast)		
la saucisse de Francfort	frankfurter	la côtelette de porc	pork chop
le jambon	ham	la saucisse	sausage
le hamburger	hamburger	le bifteck	steak
le hot dog	hot dog	la dinde	turkey
le gigot de mouton	leg of lamb		

Fruits de mer — Seafood

la carpe	carp	la sardine	sardine
la morue	cod	la crevette	shrimp
le carrelet	flounder	la raie	skate
le hareng	herring	la sole	sole
la langouste	lobster	la truite	trout
le saumon	salmon	le thon	tuna

VOCABULARY

Fruits — Fruits

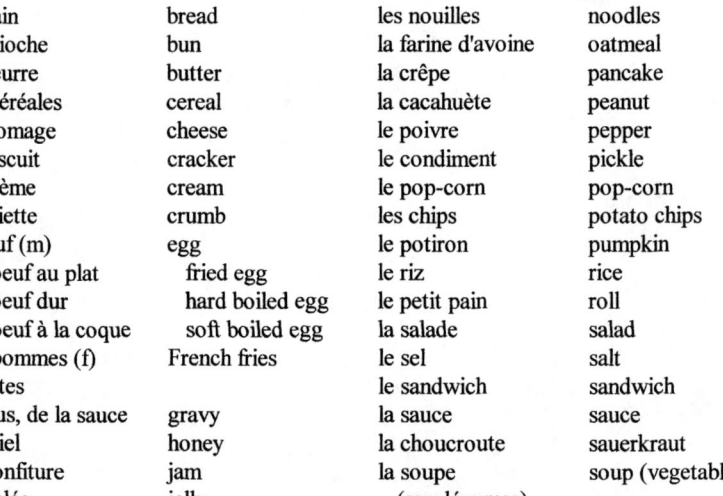

la pomme	apple
la compote de pommes	applesauce
l'abricot (m)	apricot
la banane	banana
la baie	berry
la myrtille	blueberry
la cerise	cherry
la noix de coco	coconut
le grain de raisin	grape
le pamplemousse	grapefruit
la grappe de raisin	grapes (bunch)
le citron	lemon
l'orange (f)	orange
la pêche	peach
la poire	pear
l'ananas (m)	pineapple
la prune	plum
le pruneau	prune
le raisin sec	raisin
la framboise	raspberry
la fraise	strawberry
la mandarine	tangerine

Autre nourriture — Other Food

le pain	bread
la brioche	bun
le beurre	butter
les céréales	cereal
le fromage	cheese
le biscuit	cracker
la crème	cream
la miette	crumb
l'oeuf (m)	egg
l'oeuf au plat	fried egg
l'oeuf dur	hard boiled egg
l'oeuf à la coque	soft boiled egg
les pommes (f) frites	French fries
du jus, de la sauce	gravy
le miel	honey
la confiture	jam
la gelée	jelly
la sauce tomate	ketchup
la purée de pommes de terre	mashed potatoes
le chocolat au lait	milk chocolate
la moutarde	mustard
les nouilles	noodles
la farine d'avoine	oatmeal
la crêpe	pancake
la cacahuète	peanut
le poivre	pepper
le condiment	pickle
le pop-corn	pop-corn
les chips	potato chips
le potiron	pumpkin
le riz	rice
le petit pain	roll
la salade	salad
le sel	salt
le sandwich	sandwich
la sauce	sauce
la choucroute	sauerkraut
la soupe (aux légumes)	soup (vegetable)
le spaghetti	spaghetti
le ragoût	stew
le sirop	syrup
le pain grillé	toast
le vinaigre	vinegar

VOCABULARY

Ustensiles / Utensils

la bouteille	bottle	le pot	pot
le bol	bowl	la casserole	saucepan
la tasse	cup	la soucoupe	saucer
l'assiette à dessert	dessert plate	la poêle	skillet
la fourchette	fork	l'assiette creuse	soup plate
le verre	glass	la cuillère	spoon
la bouilloire	kettle	le sucre	sugar
le couteau	knife	la nappe	tablecloth
la serviette	napkin	la cuillère à bouche	tablespoon
la cruche, la carafe	pitcher	la théière	teapot
l'assiette (f)	plate	la petite cuillère	teaspoon
le plat	platter	le plateau	tray

Maison / House

le grenier	attic	le corridor	hallway
la porte de derrière	back door	le tuyau	hose
le sous-sol, la cave	basement	la cuisine	kitchen
la salle de bains	bathroom	la pelouse	lawn
la chambre à coucher	bedroom	l'arroseuse à jet tournant	lawn sprinkler
le plafond	ceiling	le salon	living room
la cheminée	chimney	la boîte aux lettres	mail box
le bureau	den	le toit	roof
la salle à manger	dining room	l'escalier (m)	stair
la salle de séjour	family room	la marche	step
la clôture	fence	les W.C., les toilettes	toilet
le plancher	floor	la buanderie	utility room
la porte d'entrée	front door	le mur	wall
le jardin	garden	la fenêtre	window
la porte	gate	la cour	yard

Habitations / Dwellings

l'appartement (m)	apartment	le châlet	country house
la maison sans étage	bungalow	l'hôtel	hotel
la cabine	cabin	la tente	tent
l'ensemble (m) immoblier	condominium	la roulotte	trailer, mobile home

VOCABULARY

Cuisine — Kitchen

le tablier	apron	la lavette	mop
le balai	broom	le four	oven
le placard	broom closet	le seau	pail
le cabinet	cabinet	la marmite	pot (large)
l'horloge (f), la pendule	clock	la cocotte-minute	pressure cooker
		le frigo, le réfrigérateur	refrigerator
la machine à laver	clothes washer		
l'ordinateur	computer	la machine à coudre	sewing machine
le comptoir	counter		
l'armoire (m)	cupboard	l'évier (m)	sink
la lessive	detergent	l'éponge (f)	sponge
le torchon	dish cloth	le tabouret	stool
le lave-vaisselle	dish washer	le fourneau, la cuisinière	stove
l'essuie-meubles (m)	dust cloth		
la pelle	dust pan	la passoire	strainer
le fouet à oeufs	egg beater	la table	table
le batteur	electric beater	le grille-pain	toaster
l'entonnoir (m)	funnel	l'aspirateur (m)	vacuum cleaner
le fer à repasser	iron	la cire	wax (furniture)
la planche à repasser	ironing board		
le four à micro-ondes	microwave oven		

Salle de bains — Bathroom

l'aspirine (f)	aspirin	la lame de rasoir	razor blade
la serviette de bain	bath towel	le rasoir (électrique)	razor (electric)
la baignoire	bathtub	le savon à barbe	shaving soap
l'eau de cologne	cologne	le lavabo	sink
le gant de toilette	face cloth	le savon	soap
la crème	face cream	les Kleenex	tissues
le rouge à lèvres	lipstick	les toilettes	toilet
le vernis à ongles	nail polish	le papier hygiénique	toilet paper
l'essuie-tout	paper towel	la brosse à dents	toothbrush
le parfum	perfume	la pâte dentifrice	toothpaste
la poudre	powder		

VOCABULARY

Chambre à coucher — Bedroom

le fauteuil	armchair	le matelas	mattress
le lit	bed	le miroir, la glace	mirror
le couvre-lit	bedspread	l'oreiller (m)	pillow
la table de nuit	bedside table	le coussin	pillow (throw)
la couverture	blanket	la prise de courant	plug/electric outlet
le store	blind	le poster	poster
le tapis	carpet	l'édredon (m)	quilt
la chaise	chair	la chaise à bascule	rocking chair
le réveil	clock (alarm)	l'abat-jour	shade
le cintre	coat hanger	le drap	sheet
le rideau	curtain	le volet	shutter
la commode	dresser	le stéréo	stereo
la lampe	lamp	le magnétophone	tape recorder

Salon — Living Room

le climatiseur	air-conditioner	le bureau	desk
l'étagère (f)	book shelf	la cheminée, l'âtre (m)	fireplace
la bibliothèque	bookcase		
le divan	couch	le piano	piano
le sofa, le canapé	couch	le tableau	picture
le lecteur de CD	CD player	la radio	radio

Outils — Tools

la fourche	fork	la scie	saw
le marteau	hammer	les ciseaux (m)	scissors
le tuyau d'arrosage	hose	la vis	screw
l'échelle (f)	ladder	le tournevis	screwdriver
la tondeuse	lawn mower	la pelle	shovel
le clou	nail	la bêche	spade
l'écrou (m)	nut	la truelle	trowel
les pinces (f. pl)	pliers	l'étau (m)	vise
le rateau	rake	la brouette	wheelbarrow
le papier de verre	sandpaper	la clé	wrench

VOCABULARY

Voiture — The Car

l'accélérateur (m)	accelerator	le rétroviseur	(driving) mirror
les freins (m)	brakes	la vitre arrière	rear window
le pare-chocs	bumper	le siège	seat
le tableau de bord	dashboard	le démarreur	starter
la portière	door	le volant	steering wheel
le moteur	engine	la visière	sunvisor
la boîte à gants	glove compartment	le pneu	tire
le phare	headlight	le coffre	trunk
la capote	hood	la roue	wheel
le klaxon	horn	le pare-brise	windshield
l'allumage (m)	ignition	l'essuie (m) glace	windshield wiper
le cric	jack		

Magasins — Stores

la boulangerie	bakery	la poissonnerie	fish store
la banque	bank	la fleuriste	florist
le coiffeur pour hommes	barber shop	le magasin de meubles	furniture store
le salon de beauté	beauty shop	la station d'essence	gas station
le coiffeur	beauty shop	l'épicerie (f)	grocery store
la boucherie	butcher shop	la quincaillerie	hardware store
le teinturerie	cleaners	la bijouterie	jewelry store
le magasin de vêtements	clothing store	la blanchisserie	laundromat
la laiterie	dairy store	la scierie	lumber yard
le grand magasin	department store	la pépinière	nursery
la pharmacie	drug store	le magasin de chaussures	shoe store
		le magasin de jouets	toy store

Métiers — Occupations

l'astronaute	astronaut	le boucher	butcher
la gardiennne d'enfants	baby sitter	le charpentier	carpenter
		le chauffeur	chauffeur
le boulanger	baker	la femme de ménage	cleaning woman
le conducteur	bus driver		

VOCABULARY

la cuisinière	cook	le pasteur	minister
le flic	cop	le mannequin	model
le laitier	dairy man	l'infirmier (m)	nurse
la laitière	dairy woman	l'infirmière (f)	nurse
le charcutier	deli shop owner	le peintre	painter
le dentiste	dentist	le pharmacien	pharmacist
le docteur	doctor	le pilote	pilot
l'ingénieur	engineer	l'agent de police	policeman
le fermier	farmer	la femme agent	policewoman
le pompier	fireman	le père, le prêtre	priest
le garagiste	garage mechanic	le pilote de course	race car driver
l'éboueur	garbage man	le marin	sailor
le jardinier	gardiner	le/la secrétaire	secretary
l'épicier	grocer	le chausseur	shoe store man
la coiffeuse	hairdresser	le chauffeur de taxi	taxi driver
le quincailler	hardware store man		
la femme d'intérieur	housewife	le maître	teacher
		la maîtresse	teacher
le bijoutier	jeweler	le mécanicien	train engineer
l'avocat (m)	lawyer	l'ouvreur (m)	usher
l'avocate (f)	lawyer	l'ouvreuse (f)	usherette
le bibliothécaire (m)	librarian	le garçon (Garçon!)	waiter (Waiter!)
la bibliothécaire (f)	librarian	la serveuse (Mademoiselle!)	waitress (Waitress!)
la bonne	maid		
le facteur	mailman	le gardien de zoo	zoo keeper
le marchand	merchant		

Insectes   **Insects**

la fourmi	ant	le moucheron	gnat
le bourdon	bumblebee	la sauterelle	grasshopper
le papillon de jour	butterfly	l'abeille (f)	honey bee
la chenille	caterpillar	la bête à bon Dieu	lady bug
la cigale	cicada	le moustique	mosquito
la blatte	cockroach	le papillon de nuit	moth
le grillon	cricket	la mante religieuse	praying mantis
la libellule	dragonfly	l'araignée (f)	spider
la puce	flea	la guêpe	wasp
la mouche	fly		

VOCABULARY

Arbres   Trees

le pommier	apple	le poirier	pear
le bouleau	birch	le pin	pine
le cerisier	cherry	le prunier	plum
l'arbre (m) fruitier	fruit tree	le peuplier	poplar
la ciguë	hemlock	le séquoia	sequoia
l'érable (m)	maple	le sapin	spruce
le chêne	oak	le saule	willow

Animaux   Animals

l'ours (m)	bear	le lama	llama
le taureau	bull	la taupe	mole
le chameau	camel	le singe	monkey
le chat/ la chatte	cat	la souris	mouse
la vache	cow	le boeuf	ox
le crocodile	crocodile	le cochon	pig
le daim	deer	le porcelet	piglet
le chien	dog	le poney	pony
l'ane (m)	donkey	le chiot	puppy
l'éléphant (m)	elephant	le lapin	rabbit
le faon	fawn	le raton laveur	raccoon
le renard	fox	le rat	rat
le caniche	French poodle	le renne	reindeer
la grenouille	frog	le coq	rooster
la girafe	giraffe	le phoque	seal
la chèvre	goat	le mouton	sheep
le gorille	gorilla	le serpent	snake
le cochon d'inde	guinea pig	l'écureuil (m)	squirrel
l'hamster (m)	hamster	le tigre	tiger
l'hippopotame (m)	hippotamus	la tortue de mer	turtle
le cheval	horse	la baleine	whale
l'agneau (m)	lamb	le loup	wolf
le léopard	leopard	le ver (de terre)	worm (earth)
le lion	lion	le zèbre	zebra

VOCABULARY

Oiseaux **Birds**

le merle	blackbird	le hibou	owl
le rouge-gorge bleu	bluebird	le perroquet	parrot
le canari	canary	le paon	peacock
le cardinal	cardinal	le pélican	pelican
le poussin	chick	le pingouin	penguin
le poulet	chicken	le faisan	pheasant
le corbeau	crow	le pigeon	pigeon
le canard	duck	le corbeau	raven
le caneton	duckling	le rouge-gorge	robin
l'aigle (m)	eagle	la mouette	seagull
l'oie (f)	goose	le moineau	sparrow
l'oison	gosling	la cigogne	stork
le colibri	hummingbird	l'hirondelle (f)	swallow
l'alouette (f)	lark	le cygne	swan
le rossignol	nightingale	le dindon	turkey
l'autruche (f)	ostrich	le pivert	woodpecker

Fleurs **Flowers**

l'azalée (f)	azalea	le lis	lily
le bouton-d'or	buttercup	le muguet	lily of the valley
l'oeillet (m)	carnation	le mimosa	mimosa
le chrysanthème	chrysanthemum	l'orchidée (f)	orchid
le coucou	cowslip	la pensée	pansy
le crocus	crocus	la pivoine	peony
la jonquille	daffodil	le pétunia	petunia
le dahlia	dahlia	le rhododendron	rhododendron
la marguerite	daisy	la rose	rose
le pissenlit	dandelion	le tournesol	sunflower
le gardénia	gardenia	le pois de senteur	sweet pea
le géranium	geranium	la tulipe	tulip
l'iris (m)	iris	la violette	violet
le lilas	lilac		

VOCABULARY

Le long de la route   Along the Road

l'aéroport (m)	airport	le moto-scooter	motorscooter
la panne	breakdown	garer	to park
le pont	bridge	le piéton	pedestrian
le bâtiment	building	le bureau de poste	post office
l'immeuble (m)	apartment building	le chemin, la route	road
l'immeuble de bureaux	office building	le trottoir	sidewalk
l'autobus (de l'école)	bus (school)	le poteau indicateur	sign post
		l'auto-neige	snow mobile
l'autogare	bus station	la limitation de vitesse	speed limit
l'arrêt	bus stop		
la voiture	car	la voiture de course	sports car
le lave-voiture	car-wash		
l'église (f)	church	la rue	street
le coin	corner	le réverbère	street light
le bord du trottoir	curb	le taxi	taxi
l'autoroute (f)	expressway	la cabine téléphonique	telephone booth
l'usine (f)	factory		
la clôture	fence	le poteau téléphonique	telephone pole
le champ	field		
le poste de pompiers	fire house	la voie	track (railroad)
		la circulation	traffic
la bouche d'incendie	fire plug	le rond point	traffic circle
		le bouchon	traffic jam
le pneu crevé	flat tire	le feu	traffic light
l'haie (f)	hedge	le train	train
la route	highway	la gare	train station
(faire de) l'auto-stop	hitch-hiking	le camion	truck
		la voiture de dépannage	tow truck
la maison	house		
la voie	lane	le tunnel	tunnel
la boîte aux lettres	mail box	la camionnette	van
le vélomoteur	moped		
la motocyclette	motorbike, motor cycle		

PRONUNCIATION GUIDE

CONSONANTS

b, d, f, k, l, m, n, p, q, v have the same sound as in English.

c has the sound of *k* as in the word *kind* at the end of a word, before a consonant or before a, o, u. For example: clair (*klair*); carte (*kahrt*).

has the sound of *s* as in *seem* before e, i, y or when softened by a cedilla (ç) before a, o, u. For example: morceau (*mawhr-soh*); ça (*sah*).

ch similar to English *sh* as in *dish*. For example: toucher (*too-shay*).

g hard *g* as in the word *good*, before consonants or a, o, u. For example: glande (*glawnd*); garage (*gah-razh*).

as *s* in *treasure*, before e, i, y. For example: gentil (*zhawn-tee*).

gn as *ni* in opinion. For example: signe (*seen-yuh*).

h never pronounced.

PRONUNCIATION GUIDE

j as *s* in *treasure*. For example: jaune (*zhohn*).

r similar to a soft gargle. For example: rapide (*rah-peed*).

s similar to English *s*, but like the sound of an English *z* between two vowels. For example: saisir (*seh-zeer*).

t same sound as in English except when found in combination with ion, ieu, ien. In such cases *t* is pronounced like the English *s*. For example: attention (*ah-tawng-s'yohng*).

x between two vowels has the sound of *ggs* as in eggs. For example: exact (*eggs-akt*). occasionally the sound of *ss* as in six (*sees*).

VOWELS

FRENCH SPELLING	PHONETIC SOUND	DESCRIPTIONS	EXAMPLES
a, â	ah	*a* as in *farm*	p<u>a</u>p<u>a</u>
a	ah	*a* as in *sat*	t<u>a</u>sse, s<u>a</u>lle
ai	eh	*e* as in *rest*	s<u>ai</u>sir
ail, aille	igh	*igh* as in *high*	trav<u>aille</u>
aim, ain, ein, im, in	ahng	nasalized *a* as in *sat*	<u>aim</u>able, m<u>ain</u>, pl<u>ein</u>, <u>im</u>meuble, jard<u>in</u>
am, an, em, en	awng	nasalized *a* as in *farm*	t<u>am</u>bour, m<u>an</u>teau, <u>em</u>barquer, comm<u>en</u>cer
au, eau	oh	*o* as in *no*	<u>au</u> revoir, bat<u>eau</u>
e	uh	*e* as the unstressed *e* in *the*	l<u>e</u>, t<u>e</u>, d<u>e</u>
é	ay	*a* as in *may*	b<u>é</u>b<u>é</u>
è, ê, ei	eh	*e* as in *wet*	m<u>è</u>re, <u>ê</u>tre, n<u>ei</u>ge

PRONUNCIATION GUIDE

eil, eille	ay-yuh (with a soft yuh added at the end of the word)	*a* as in *may*	ort<u>eil</u>, or<u>eille</u>
eu, oeu	uh	*ue* as in *fuel*	f<u>eu</u>
i, î	ee	*ee* as in *see*	an<u>i</u>mal
ien	y'ehng	*yan* as in *yankee*	b<u>ien</u>
ille	ee (with a soft yuh added at the end of the word)	*ee* as in *see*	fi<u>lle</u>
o, ô	oh	*o* as in *no*	d<u>o</u>s, dr<u>ô</u>le
o	awh	*o* as in *moss*	p<u>o</u>rte
oi, oî	wah	*wa* as in *watch*	t<u>oi</u>, b<u>oî</u>te
oin	wahng	*an* as in *answer* preceded by *w*	bes<u>oin</u>
om, on	ohng	nasalized *o* as in *coffee*	<u>o</u>rnbre, t<u>on</u>
ou, oû	oo	*oo* as in *food*	p<u>ou</u>pée, c<u>oû</u>ter
u, û	ew	*ew* as in *few*	t<u>u</u>, am<u>u</u>ser
ui	wee	*wee* as in *week*	br<u>ui</u>t

151

INDEX

INDEX

A

to abandon	quitter 80
(to be) able	pouvoir 70,77,101
to add	ajouter 55
adjusted	ajusté/e 92
to admit	entrer 36
All aboard!	Embarquez! (boat) 80
All aboard!	En voiture! (train) 88
(to be) afraid	avoir peur 48
after	après 55,124
afternoon	l'après-midi 64,91
again	encore 99
air mattress	le matelas pneumatique 95
airplane	l'avion 59,74
airport	l'aeroport 59
alarm clock	le reveil 22
(to be) all right	s'arranger 48
almost	presque 107,112
alphabet	l'alphabet 126
(all) alone	tout/e seul/e 23, 68
alone	tranquil/le 40
aloud	à haute voix 64
angel	l'ange 98
(to be) angry	se mettre en colère 48
animal	l'animal 75
another	autre 45,120
answer	la réponse 49,63
to answer	répondre 62
anyone	quelqu'un/e 13,27,65
apple	la pomme 27
appointment	le rendez-vous 92
to appreciate	apprécier 68
arm	le bras 32,115
around	autour de 85,87
to arrive	arriver 88,99
artist	l'artisan 66
to ask	demander 37,44,74
to ask (question)	poser 61
(to be) asleep	endormi/e 114
attic	le grenier 94
(to be) awake	réveiller 114
awful	affreux 118
awful	effroyable 104

B

baby	le bébé 35,46,68
back	le dos 20
backwards	en arrière 87
back-yard	l'arrière-cour 76,94
bacon	le lard 26
bad	mauvais/e 28,118
bag	le sac 128
bait	l'amorce 93
to bake	cuire 63
to bake	faire 54,55
bakery	la boulangerie 56
baking powder	la levure 55
balance	l'équilibre 78
ball	la balle 34,77,78,89
balloon	le ballon 86
banana	la banane 27
bandaid	le pansement 115
to bang	battre 35
bank	la banque 57
to bark	aboyer 75
baseball	le baseball 77
bat	la batte 77
bath	le bain 19, 21
bathroom	la salle de bains 17,50
battery	la batterie 76
beach	la plage 94,95,109
to beat	fouetter 55
beautiful	beau/ belle 66,96,110,116
because	parce que 44
bed	le lit 53,54,112,113,115
bed time	l'heure du coucher 111
before	avant de 30,43,56,112
to begin	commencer 119
to behave	se tenir 47
behind	derrière 18,77
behind	en arrière 70
bell	la cloche 35
bell	le timbre (bike) 78
to belong	aller 42
to belong	appartenir 21

INDEX

B (cont.)

beside	à côté de 85
best	le mieux 103
better	mieux 47,68,103,115
bicycle	le vélo 78,79
bicycling	le cyclisme 78
big	grand/e 33, 67
bird	l'oiseau 81,96
birthday	l'anniversaire 15,109
birthday party	la fête d'anniversaire 109
to bite	ronger 24
bitter	amer/ amère 28
blanket	la couverture 95
to bless	bénir 15, 114
blindman's buff	colin-maillard 89
block	le cube (toy) 37,89
blouse	la blouse 23
to blow	se moucher (nose) 49
to blow out	souffler 110
to blow up	gonfler (inflate) 86
board	la planche 58,94
board game	le jeu de société 79
boat	le bateau 59,80
book	le livre 112
boot	la chaussure 97
(to be) bored	s'ennuyer 73
to borrow	emprunter 76
both	tout les deux 77
(at the) bottom	au fond 94
box	la boîte 40,41
boy	le garçon 67,128
braces	l'appareil dentaire 92
to brake	freiner 79
bread	le pain 29
to break	casser 40
breakfast	le petit déjeuner 25,30
breath	le souffle 117
to breathe	respirer 49
brilliant	brillant/e 66
to bring	apporter 44,50,95
brother	le frère 33
to browse	feuilleter 83
brush	la brosse 18,24
to brush	brosser 18,24

B (cont.)

bubble	la bulle 77
to build	bâtir 96,120
to bump	faire une bosse 48
buoy	la bouée 96
to burn oneself	se brûler 42
bus	le bus 92
busy	occupé/e 37
butcher (shop)	la boucherie 56
butter	le beurre 55
to button	bouttoner 23
to buy	acheter 69,70,71

C

CD	le CD 93
cabinet	le cabinet 85
cake	le gâteau 110
to call	appeler 26
to call	téléphoner 93
to calm oneself	se calmer 48
camel	le chameau 75
to camp	camper 81
camp site	le camping 81
camping	le camping 81
Can I...?	Puis-je...? 29,64,76
candle	la bougie 110
car	la voiture 76,92,93
card	la carte 89
(to be) careful	faire attention 27,43,57
(to be) careful	prendre garde 43,77
carefully	doucement 42
carefully	soigneusement 29,82
carriage	la voiture d'enfant 90
carrot	la carrotte 26
to carry	porter 44
cartoon	le dessin animé 91
castle	le château 96
cat	le chat 40,58,127
to catch	attraper 77,94
caterpillar	le chenille 57
cattle truck	le wagon à bestiaux 88

C (cont.)

caught	saisi 94
cereal	la céréale 25,27
chair	la chaise 46
chairlift	le remonte-pente 97
change	la monnaie 72
to change	changer 22
chapter	le chapitre 62
cheaper	meilleur marché 70
to check	vérifier 76
check-out	la caisse 71
check-up	le bilan de santé 35
cheese	le fromage 28
chest	la poitrine 115
to chew	mâchoir 28
chicken pox	la varicelle 115
chore	le travail domestique 92
Christmas	le Noël 15, 130
circle	le cercle 82,86
to clap	claquer 35
to clap	frapper 89
class	la classe 60
clay	la pâte à modeler 82
clean	proper 17,19
to clean	nettoyer 18,68,82
to clean house	faire le ménage 53
to clean up	ranger 54
cleaning	le nettoyage 55
clear	clair/e 94
to clear	desservir (table) 53
clearly	clairement 47,63
to climb	grimper 46,77
to climb	monter 42
close	prêt de 26
to close	fermer 23, 85,113
clothes	les vêtements 56,112
cloud	le nuage 116
clown	le clown 90
coat	le manteau 24,71,117
coffee	le café 28
cold	froid/e 19,95,98
cold (n)	le rhume 115
coliseum	le colisée 92
to color	colorer 81

C (cont.)

comb	le peigne 24
to comb	se peigner 24
to come	venir 35,39,45
to come back	rentrer 16
to come back	revenir 38,99
to come down	descendre 42
to come in	entrer 45
Come on!	Allons! 51
comic-book	la bande dessinée 94
to complain	se plaindre 107
complaint	la plainte 52
computer	l'ordinateur 82
control tower	la tour de contrôle 74
to cook	préparer 54
cookie	le biscuit 63
cookie	le gâteau sec 54,55,124
cool	frais/ fraîche 117
correct	corriger 63
to cost	coûter 71,97
cough	la toux 115
to cough	tousser 115
Could you...?	Pourrais-tu...? 43
to count	compter 72,84,124
covered	couvert 58
cowboy	le cowboy 74
crayon	le crayon gras 65
crayon	le pastel 50,81
crazy	fou/folle 51,102
to cross	traverser 43
(to be) cross	mauvaise humeur 47
to crow	chanter 75
crumb	la miette 28
to cry	pleurer 48,107
cup	la tasse 83
curls	les boucles 67
to cut	couper 27,29,43,110
to cut (lawn)	tondre la pelouse 57
to cut out	découper 82
cute	mignon/ne 67

INDEX

D

daddy	papa 37
to dance	danser 66
dangerous	dangereux/ use 58
dark	le noir 51
dark	sombre 118
Darn!	Zut! 100
day	la journée 116,118
(Oh) dear!	Mon Dieu ! 100
delicious	délicieux/ use 30
to deliver	délivrer 88
dentist	le dentiste 92
department store	le grand magazin 56
dessert	le dessert 28
diaper	la couche 22
difference	la différence 63
to dig	creuser 57
dinner	le dîner 26,30,54,90
dirt	la terre 77
dirty	sale 18, 40
to dirty	salir 45
dish	l'assiette 44
to disobey	désobéir 39
to divide	diviser 110
diving board	le plongeoir 77
dizziness	le vertige 114
to do, make	faire 39,43,44,45,47,50 73,101,102,103
to dock	amarrer 80
doctor	le docteur 74
doctor	le médicin 35
dog	le chien 40,58,75
doll	la poupée 74,83
door	la porte 40
Down with !	à bas! 64
downstairs	en bas 45,50
to drag	trainer 83
to draw	dessiner 66,81,82,96
to draw	faire un dessin 82
dream	le rêve 113
to dream	rêver 32
dress	la robe 67
to dress	habiller 83
to dress oneself	s'habiller 23
dresser	la commode 24

D (cont.)

drink	la boisson 96
to drink	boire 27,30
to drive	conduire 76
to drive crazy	se rendre folle 51
driveway	l'allée 87
to drop	laisser tomber 43
drug store	la pharmacie 56
drum	le tambour 35
to dry	essuyer (dishes) 53
to dry (oneself)	se sêcher 20,48
dull	émoussé/e 87
dust	la poussière 54
to dust	épousseter 54
to dust	essuyer 54
dust cloth	le chiffon à poussière 54
to dye	teindre 93

E

e-mail	e-mail 63
each	chacun/ ne 69
ear	l'oreille 18,33
early	tôt 113
to earn	mériter 65
Easter	Pâques 15
easy	facile 103
easy	simple 65
to eat	manger 25,26,27,28,30, 42,66,98,124
to eat out	dîner en ville 92
elbow	le coude 26
elephant	l'éléphant 75
elevator	l'ascenseur 70
to empty	vider 20,45
enough	assez de 77,85,125
equipment	l'équipment 97
error	l'erreur 82
escalator	l'escalier roulant 70
everbody	tout le monde 21,102
everything	chaque chose 41
example	l'opération 63

156

E (cont.)

to excuse	excuser 15
expensive	cher, chère 70
to explain	expliquier 63
extra	supplémentaire 64
extraordinary	extraordinaire 104
eye	l'oeil 113
eyes	les yeux 33,35,67, 81,85,113

F

face	la figure 18
face	le visage 18, 19, 29, 114
(to make) faces	faire grimaces 49
face cloth	le gant de toilette 20
fair	franc 79
fair	juste 79
to fall	tomber 41, 101
fare	le prix 88
fast	vite 27,79,97
fast food	à service rapide 92
father	papa 54,74
faucet	le robinet 19
fault	en tort 101
fault	la faute 101
fax	la télécopie 83
to feed	donner manger 28,58,83
to feel	se sentir 114
to feel	toucher 61
fever	la fièvre 114
fidgety	la bougeotte 114
to fight	battre 39
to fill	faire plein 76
to fill	remplir 19
finally	enfin 23
to find	trouver 65
finger	le doight 43,115,123
fingernail	l'ongle 18,24
to finish	finir 62,63,92
Fire!	Au feu! 83
fire engine	la voiture de pompier 83

F (cont.)

fish	le poisson 94
to fish	pêcher 94
fishing rod	la canne à pêche 93
to fit	aller bien 86
to fix	faire 26
flat (flavor)	fade 28
floor	le plancher 42,83
floss	la soie dentaire 18
flour	la farine 55
flower	la fleur 77,92
to flush	tirer 18
to fly	voler 96
fog	le brouillard 119
to fold	plier 20,82
to follow	suivre 50
food	la nourriture 28,29
foot	le pied 22,23,35,42,78, 115,118
football	le soccer 87
to forget	oublier 18,42,49,58,82
fork	la fourchette 27
form	la forme 98
to form	former 82
free	libre 74
to freeze	geler 119
French	le français 16
friend	l'ami/e 110
friend	la camarade 74
to frighten	faire peur 31
in front of	devant 85
frown	le froncement 107
full	plein/e 118
fun	amusant 91,93
funny	drôle 103

G

game	le jeu 110
garage	le garage 76
garbage	l'ordure 58
garbage pail	la poubelle 58

INDEX

G (cont.)

garden	le jardin 57
gardening	le jardinage 62,65
gasoline	l'essence 75
gas station	le poste d'essence 59
to gather	ramasser 99
gently	doucement 83
gently	gentiment 46,85
to get	chercher 78,112
to get (become)	devenir 96,113
to get	prendre 25
to get (capture)	attraper 84
to get down	descendre 46
to get dressed	s'habiller 22,62
to get in	faire entrer 93
girl	la fille 67
to give	donner 36,37,68
to give up	donner la langue...90
to give up	quitter 68
glad	content/e 61
glad	heureux/use 63, 100
gland	la glande 114
glass	le verre 29
glasses (eye)	les lunettes 96
glove	le gant 23
to go	aller 33, 87
Go ahead!	Vas-y ! 51
to go (engine)	marcher 76
to go	continuer 39
to go back	se recoucher (to bed) 113
to go down	descendre 50
to go first	passer d'abord 50
to go for a walk	se promener 36,90
to go get	aller chercher 112
to go out	s'aller 38
to go out	partir 23,37,99
to go out	sortir 50, 52,74, 91,92
to go to bed	se coucher 112
to go to sleep	endormir 113
to go upstairs	monter 112
goal	le but 87
God	Dieu 14,108,114
good	bon/ ne 67
(Be) good!	Sois sage ! 48
good	bien 49
"Gotcha!"	Attrapé ! 84

G (cont.)

to grab	saisir 44
grandma	la grand-mère 35,50
gray	gris/e 118
green light	le feu vert 43
grocery store	l'épicerie 56
ground	le sol 58
ground	la terre 43
to grow	pousser 57
grown up	être grand/e 110

H

hair	les cheveux 21,92
half-way	mi-chemin 42
hammer	le marteau 94
to hammer	enfoncer 58
hand	la main 19,22,27,34,35, 36,44, 67,87
Hands off!	à bas ! 40
handkerchief	le mouchoir 89
handle	la poignée 43
handlebar	le guidon 78
handsome	beau 67
hang gliding	le delta-plane 93
to hang up	pendre 20, 112
hanger	le cintre 112
to happen	arriver 46,102
hard	dur/e 83, 97
hardware store	la quincaillerie 57
hat	le chapeau 23, 110
to have	avoir 26,34,44
to have a good time	s'amuser 73,99
to have just	venir de + inf. 95
to have off	avoir congé 65
to have to	devoir 61
head	la tête 32
health	la santé 15
to hear	entendre 31
head set	le casque 51
heavy	lourd/e 113
Hello!	Allô ! 13
Hello!	Salut !13

H (cont.)

Help!	Au secours! 83, 101
help	l'aide 68
to help	aider 24,44,50,53,55,58,87
to help oneself	se servir 26
here is	voici 34
to hide	cacher 84
hide and seek	cache-cache 84
to hit	frapper 77,78
hill	la colline 97
hobby	le passe-temps favori 65
to hold	tenir 32,34,43,77,85,86,127
to hold onto	tenir 90
hole	le trou 57
hole punch	la perforeuse 62
homework	les devoirs 62,63,64
hook	l'hameçon 93
hoop	le cerceau 84, 89
to hop	sauter 75
to hope	espérer 105
hot	chaud/e 19,117
hot dog	le hot dog 27
hour	l'heure 55
house	la maison 53
how	comment 14
how far	jusqu'où 98
how much	combien 71,97
how well	comme 66
hump	la bosse 75
(to be) hungry	avoir faim 98
to hurry	se presser 37
to hurry	se dépêcher 41
to hurt	faire mal 35, 36, 48, 115
to hurt	se blesser 79
to hurt	avoir mal 115

I

ice cream	la glace 110
immediately	tout de suite 50
indian	l'indien 74
inside	à l'intérieur 38,76
interesting	intéressant/e 103
to invite	inviter 74, 110
to iron	repasser 55

J

jacket	la veste 23
jammed	bloqué/e 62
jelly fish	la méduse 95
to jog	faire du jogging 86
joke	la blague 104
juice	le jus 29
to jump	sauter 41,77,85,86
to just	venir de + inf. 60

K

kangaroo	le kangourou 75
to keep	garder 68
to keep on	continuer 68, 78
to keep an eye	tenir l'oeil 96
to kick	frapper 34
to kick	lancer 87
kind	agréable 104
kind	gentil/ le 46
to kiss	embrasser 113
kitchen	la cuisine 42
kite	le cerf-volant 86
knee	le genou 20
knife	le couteau 27,43
to knock down	démolir 89
knot	le noeud 24
to know	connaître 33
to know	savoir 102, 110
label	l'étiquette 71
to land	atterrir 75,96
language	la language 47
lap	les genoux 32
large	large 71, 75
last	le dernier/ère 86
late	en retard 52,96
late	tard 52
later	plus tard 21,38
to laugh	rire 108
laundry	le linge 55
lawn	la pelouse 57
to lay down	allonger 83
to lead	mener 86

INDEX

L (cont.)

leader	le chef 84
to look good	aller bien 72
leaf	la feuille 57,58
to leak	dégonfler 86
to lean	pencher 40
to learn	apprendre 64
to leave	laisser 21,40,90,107
to leave	partir 98
to leave	sortir 77
left (remaining)	rester 27
leg	la jambe 32,80
lesson	la leçon 65
Let go!	Lâche prise! 32
Let me...	Fais-moi... 71
to let, allow	laisser 24,45,81
Let's go!	Allons! 51,91
Let's go play!	Allons jouer! 120
letter	la lettre 126,127
library	la bibliothèque 57, 92
to lie down	se coucher 46,75,95
life boat	le canot de sauvetage 80
to lift	lever 87
light	la lumière 20,21,51,113
lightning	l'éclair 119
to like	aimer 21,36
to like (be pleasing to)	se plaire 68, 70
like this	comme ça 82,101
line	le fil 55
line	la ligne 94
line	la queue 72
lipstick	le rouge à lèvres 24
to listen	écouter 31,47,64,93
lit	allumé/e 21
(a) little	un peu 27,28,57,64
to live	s'habiller 16
to live	vivre 22
to load up	charger 88
to lock	fermer à clé 40
Look!	Regarde! 107
Look out!	Attention! 101
to look	avoir l'air 21,24
to look (appear)	paraître 100
to look at	regarder 32,35,41,43,62, 71, 89,101,104,108,118

L (cont.)

to look for	chercher 23
to look good	aller bien 72
loose	large 71
to lose	perdre 80
(a) lot	beaucoup 65
loud	fort/e 35
to love	adorer 91
to love	aimer 34,56,113,118
to lower	abaisser 80
luck	la chance 16,104
to be lucky	avoir de la chance 104
lumber yard	le cour de débarras 59
lunch	le déjeuner 30,44,96
to have lunch	déjeuner 25

M

magazine	la revue 82
to make, do	faire 53,54,58
to make faces	faire des grimaces 49
to make up (one's mind)	décider 105
mall	la galerie marchande 91
map	la carte 62
marble (toy)	la bille 86
marina	le port de plaisance 59
marked	marqué/e 71
market	le marché 56, 69
marvelous	merveilleux/ use 104
match, game	le match 94
matches	les allumettes 42
meal	le repas 29
to mean	vouloir dire 127
meat	la viande 27
medicine	le médicament 115
to meet	rencontrer 94
to melt	fondre 120
mess	désordre 54
microwave-oven	le four micro-onde 26
milk	le lait 27,29,30

160

INDEX

M (cont.)

minus	moins 124
mirror	la glace 34,108
to miss	manquer 14,78
mistake	la faute 63
to mix	mélanger 55
mommy	maman 26,35,36,62
money	l'argent 70
mop	le balai à laver 44
more	encore 27
more	plus 103
morning	le matin 64
mouse	la souris 34
mouth	la bouche 33,34,81, 115
to move	bouger 38
to move	tourner 32
move	le tour 79
movies	le cinéma 90
music	la musique 51
must, ought	devoir 41
must	il faut 22, 38,56,57,59, 63,69,87
myself	moi-même 103

N

nail	le clou 58,94
mail file	la lime à ongles 24
name	le nom 127
napkin	la serviette 53
nasty	vilain/e 118
naughty	vilain/e 48
near	près de 42, 81
necessary	nécessaire 106
neck	le cou 18,20
to need	avoir besoin de 17,21,69,117
nervous	nerveux/ use 40
net	le filet 93
new	nouveau/ nouvelle 24,56,93,115
nice	agréable 65,95,104
nice	gentil/le 67,68,106
night	la nuit 117
no	non 15

N (cont.)

noise	le bruit 31, 37,114
nonsense	bêtise 104
nose	le nez 33
not	non 105
nothing	rien 73
now	maintenant 19,37
nurse	l'infirmière 74
nursery (plants)	la pépinière 59

O

obstacle	l'obstacle 84
oil	l'huile 76,88
on-line	en ligne 62, 82
only	seulement 71
to open	ouvrir 40,115
opening	l'ouverture 70
or	ou 45
out of gas	à sec 76
outdoors	en pleine aire 64
outside	dehors 76
outside	l'extérieur 38
oven	le four 55
over there	là bas 41,71

P

page	la page 64
pail	le sceau 95
to paint	peindre 81
pajamas	le pyjama 112
pants	le pantalon 22,24
paper	le papier 65,82
paper clip	le trombone 61
pardon	le pardon 15
park	le parc 109
party	la boum 109, 110
to pass	passer 27
password	le mot de passe 82
to paste	coller 81,82
patient (adj)	patient/e 68

INDEX

P (cont.)

to pay attention	faire attention 43
peace	la paix 101
peas	les pois 29
pebble	le caillou 49
pedal	la pédale 78
to pedal	pédaler 78
peek-a-boo	cou-cou 88
pencil	le crayon 61,65,127
perhaps	peut-être 70
permission	la permision 112
to pet	caresser 40
to pick	cueillir 77
to pick up	ramasser 40
picture	le dessin 63
picture	l'image 82,96
piece	le morceau 58,86
piece	la pièce 79
pilot	le pilot 74
pity	le dommage 104
pizza	la pizza 26
place	la place 41,124
plant	la plante 57
to plant	planter 57
plate	l'assiette 28,30
play	la pièce 92
to play	jouer 34,42,48,50,56, 68,76,77,91
to play	jouer (instrument) 66,73,74
to play fair	jouer franc 79
playground	le parc de jeux 85,91
please	s'il te plaît 15,44
plenty	beaucoup 20
pocket	la poche 45
to point	montrer du doight 127
to polish	faire briller 23
pool	la piscine 77,94
poster	le poster 61
potato	la pomme de terre 26
to pour	verser 29,55
prayer	la prière 112
to prefer	préférer 81,90
to prepare	préparer 44
present	le cadeau 110
to press	appuyer 51

P (cont.)

to pretend	prétendre 75
pretty	joli/e 67
problem	le problème 62
project	le projet 60
to promise	promettre 47
to prune	tailler 58
puddle	la flaque 118
puppet	la marionette 92
(on) purpose	esprès 47
to push	pousser 76,85,87
to put	mettre 22,26,28, 34,41,111
to put away	ranger 65,90,112
to put back	remettre 42
to put on	mettre 112
to put out	sortir 58
puzzle	le casse-tête 86

Q

to quarrel	disputer 39
(Be) quiet!	Tais-toi! 113,37
quick	vite 34
to be quiet	silence 37
to be quiet	se taisser 37
quietly	sans bruit 68

R

radio	la radio 64
rain	la pluie 118,120
to rain	pleuvoir 117
rainbow	l'arc en ciel 119
raindrop	la goutte 117
to raise	élever 108
to raise	se lever 32
to rake	ratisser 57
rattle	le hochet 32,88
to reach	tendre 37
to read	lire 55,61,62,64 111,125
ready	prêt/e 112
to ready	préparer 35
recess	la récréation 62

R (cont.)

red	rouge 93
refrigerator	le frigo 40
to remain	rester 46
to remember	se souvenir 50
to rent	louer 97
to repeat	répéter 127
to rest	reposer 98
restaurant	le restaurant 92,109
to return	rendre (an item) 69
to ride (car)	promener en voiture 93
to ride (bike)	faire du vélo 79
right	just/e 63
right	la raison 63
to rinse	se rincer 20
to ring	sonner 22, 35
rock	la pierre 44
to rock	bercer 46
to roll over	rouler 34,82,89
roller blading	patiner en ligne 93
roller skating	patiner à roulettes 93
room	la chambre 45,554,56,68,89
rooster	le coq 75
rope	la corde 86
rough	houleux/ use 95
row	canoter 80
to rub	frotter 33,48,54
rug	le tapis 42
to run	courir 78,80,86
to run(water)	couler 19
runway	la piste 75

S

sad	triste 100
to sail	mettre les voiles 80
sale	la vente 69
(on) sale	en solde 70
salesman	le vendeur 78
saleswoman	la vendeuse 71
salt	le sel 27
salty	salé/e 28
sand	le sable 88,96
to sand	sabler 58

S (cont.)

sandbox	le bac à sable 76
sandwich	le sandwich 26
sauce	la sauce 28
saw	la scie 94
to saw	scier 58
to say	dire 43, 48,103, 105,108
school bus	le car d'école 60
science	la science 61
scissors	les ciseaux 61
to score	marquer 87
scotch tape	le ruban adhésif 61
to scratch	gratter 114
screwdriver	le tournevis 58
sea	la mer 95
seashell	le coquillage 96
seat	la place 26
seat	le siège 15
to see	voir 34,35,45,81,89
seed	le grain 57
to send	envoyer 63,83
to set	mettre 53,55
to set up	dresser 81
shade	l'ombre 95
to shade	agiter 88
shampoo	le shampooing 21
to share	partager 73,95
sharp	coupant/e 43
to sharpen	aiguiser 87
to shave	raser 21
shirt	la chemise 23,45,112
shoe	le soulier 22,23,118
shoelace	le lacet 24
Shoot!	Shoote! 87
to shoot	lancer 86
to shop	faire les courses 56,69
shopping cart	le caddy 70
shore	le rivage 94
short	court/e 70
shovel	la pelle 95
to shovel	enlever 56
show	l'exposition 92
to show	montrer 45,48,62,77
sick	malade 65

S (cont.)

simple	simple 65
to sing	chanter 32,66
to sink	couler 80
sip	la goutte 28
siren	la sirène 84
sister	la soeur 33, 62,96
to sit	s'asseoir 26,32,46
size	la taille 71
skate	le patin 87
skateboarding	faire de la planche à roulettes 93
to skate	patiner 87
skating	le patinage 87
skating rink	la patinoire 87
ski	le ski 97
ski pole	le bâton de ski 97
to ski	faire du ski 96,97
to skip	sauter 64
sky	le ciel 95,117
sled	la luge 120
to sled	faire de la luge 97
sleep	le sommeil 114
to sleep	se coucher 81
to sleep	dormir 46,113,114,115
sleepy byes	faire dodo 115
sleeve	la manche 22
slide	le tobaggan 85
to slide	glisser 85,120
slippery	glissant/e 20
Slow down!	Ralentis! 41
slowly	lentement 47
small	petit/e 33
to smell	sentir 20,28
smile	le sourire 33
to smile	sourire 33,68
snack	le casse-croûte 26
snack	le goûter 30
snow	la neige 56,97,98,119,120
to snow	neiger 119
snowflake	le flocon 119
snowman	le bonhomme de neige 120
so-so	comme-çi, comme-ça 14
so much	tant de 20
so much	tellement 29

S (cont.)

soap	le savon 20
soccer	le football 64
sock	la chaussette 112
soft	mou/molle 97
something	quelque chose 113,115
(to be) sorry	désolé/e 101
to sort	séparer 55
to sound	sonner 84
soup	la soupe 29
sour	aigre 28
to spank	donner la fessée 83
to sparkle	étinceler 120
to speak	parler 16,29,47,66,81
speed boat	l'hors-bord 96
to spend (money)	dépenser 70
to spend (time)	passer 64
to spill	renvérser 29
spinach	épinards 28
spirits	l'humeur 68
spoiled	gâté/e 48
spoon	la cuiller 27
spot	le bouton 115
to spread	étendre 95
to spy	voir 89
square	le carré 82
to squeeze	presser 82
to stack	empiler 89
to stain	tacher 42
stairs	les escaliers 42
to stand	se mettre debout 20,46,68,85
Stand back!	Recule! 42
to stand in line	faire le queue 72
staple	l'agrafe 61
stapler	l'agrafeuse 61
to start	commencer 60
to start again	recommencer 64
to start (car)	démarrer 76
to stay	rester 38,70,115
steep	raid/e 97
to steer	diriger 78
step	le pas 67
step (of stairs)	la marche 42
still (adj)	tranquil/le 113

S (cont.)

Stop!	Arrête-toi! 36, 38,39,89
to stop	s'arrêter 60
storm	la tempête 119
story	l'histoire 33,55
story(fairy tale)	le conte 112
stove	le fourneau 42
straight	tout droit
to straighten	ranger 56
street	la rue 43,79,118
strong	fort/e 32
stubborn	têtu/e 48
to study	étudier 61
subway	le métro 92
sugar	le sucre 55
to suit	s'aller bien 67
summer	l'été 117
sun	le soleil 81,95,96,116
sun glasses	les lunettes de soleil 96
suntan lotion	le lait solaire 96
suspicious	soupçonneux/use 52
supposed	censé 39
to sweep	balayer 54
sweet	sucré/e 28
sweet	mignon/ ne 67
to swim	nager 62,77,94,96
swing	la balançoire 85
to swing	balancer 85
to swing	brandir 78
switch	le bouton 51
swollen	gonflé/e 114

T

table	la table 26,85
tablecloth	la nappe 53
tail	la queue 86
to take	prendre 29,107,115
to take away	emporter 44
to take care	prendre garde 41
to take a bath	prendre un bain 19,21
to take a photo	prendre un photo 33,98

S (cont.)

to take exams	passer des examens 63
to take a ride	faire une promenade en voiture 90
to take off	décoller 75
to take off	enlever 51
to take off	oter (plane) 118
to take off	déshabiller 112
to talk	parler 38,49,68
tanker	le citerne 88
taste	le goût 69
to taxi	rouler 74
tea	le thé 28
tear	la larme 48
to tear	déchirer 82
to tease	taquiner 40
teddy bear	l'ours en peluche 83
telephone	le téléphone 68
to telephone	téléphoner 13
television	la télévision 51,112
to tell	dire 17,39,45,49,100
tent	la tente 81
Thank you	Merci 14,15
then	puis 125
There!	Voilà 115
there is/ are	il y a 57,77,86
to think	penser 32,44,105
to think	songer 62
through	travers de 84
to throw	jeter 44,58,65,77
thunder	le tonnerre 119
ticket	le billet 88,97
ticktacktoe	le jeu des carrés 89
tide	la marée 94
to tidy	ranger 89
to tie	attacher 24
tight	étroit/e 71
time	le temps 22,35,62
(on) time	à l'heure 52,90
tired	fatigué/e 98,108,111
today	aujourd'hui 61,116
toe	l'orteil 20,81
together	ensemble 45

INDEX

T (cont.)

toilet	les toilettes 18
tomorrow	demain 115
tongue	la langue 115
too much	trop de 70, 79
tool	l'outil 40
tooth	le dent 18,35
toothbrush	la brosse à dents 18
top	en haut 64
top	le sommet 97
top (toy)	la toupie 86
to touch	toucher 40,42,72,87
towel	la serviette 20,68,95
towel rack	le porte-serviettes 20
tower	la tour 74
toy	le jouet 49, 73,90,107
toy	le joujou 61
toy box	la boîte à joujoux 90
traffic	la circulation 99
train	le train 88,92
trash	l'ordure 65
tree	l'arbre 77
tree house	la cabane 94
triangle	le triangle 82
(to give) trouble	déranger 39
truck	le camion 88
true	vrai 106
trunk (elephant)	la trompe 75
trust	la confiance 52
truth	la vérité 47
to try	essayer 29,45,68,71
tub	la baignoire 19,20
tummy	le ventre 33,67
turn	le tour 39
(It's your) turn	C'est à toi. 58
to turn around	tourner 42
to turn down	baisser 51
to turn off	éteindre 20,51
to turn off (faucet)	fermer 19
to turn on (faucet)	ouvrir 19
to turn on	faire marcher 51

U (cont.)

umbrella (beach)	le parasol 95
under	sous 85
underwear	les sous-vêtements 24
to understand	comprendre 48
unpleasant	mauvais/e 118
until	jusqu'à 38,39,84
unusual	rare 104
upstairs	en haut 45,50
to use	se servir 24,49,81
(to get) used to	habituer 104

V

to vacuum	passer l'aspirateur 54
vacuum cleaner	l'aspirateur 54
to visit	visiter 35
voice	la voix 66,108

W

wagon	le wagon 58,77
to wait for	attendre 38,43,102,108
to wake up	se reveiller 22, 114
to walk	marcher 35,41,66,75
to walk	promener 41,58,118
walkman	le baladeur 51
to want	vouloir 25,27,36,45
warm	chaud/e 95
to warm up	réchauffer 26,98
wash (clothing)	le lavage 53
to wash	se laver 18
to wash dishes	faire la vaisselle 53
washroom	les lavabos 72
wastebasket	la corbeille 65
Watch!	Attention! 43
to watch	regarder 59,96,112
water	l'eau 76,94
to water	arroser 57
water-ski	le ski nautique 95

166

W (cont.)

way	le chemin 45
way	le moyen 99,105
to wear	porter 23,24
weather	le temps 116
weeds	les mauvaises herbes 57
to weed	enlever les mauvaises herbes 57
Welcome!	Bienvenue! 14
well	bien 66
Well done!	Bravo! 68
wet	mouillé/e 114,118
to wet	faire mouiller 34
what	ce que 39
what	comment 107
what	quel/le 31
what	qu'est - ce que 31
when	quand 25,26,99
where	où 16,23,33,45,84
which	quel/le 115
while	pendant que 61,64,68,84
who	qui 21,33
whose	à qui 61,79,127
why	pourquoi 29,44
to win	gagner 80,100
wind	le vent 85,117
window	la fenêtre 40,89
winter	l'hiver 119
to wipe	essuyer 42

W (cont.)

wish	le voeux 110
with	avec 46,77,80
without	sans 43,50
wonderful	merveilleux/use 66
word	le mot 127
work	le travail 43
to work	travailler 23,59 61,65
would like (you)	voudrais 25,27
to write	écrire 64,66
writing	l'écriture 127
wrong	mauvais/e 23,79
wrong	la tort 63

XYZ

yard	la cour 76,77
yawn	le bâillement 111
to yawn	bâiller 111
yellow	jaune 81
yes	oui 15
yours	le tien/ne 51
yourself	toi-même 34
zipper	la fermeture éclair 23

COLOR, CUT and PASTE

A colorful, fun and easy way to get acquainted with this book is to match the pictures on the next few pages with the sentences in the text. The page number on the back of each drawing is given to help you spot the page you are looking for. An asterisk next to the appropriate sentence is also given to help you pinpoint the exact sentence. Sometimes a picture will match more than one sentence.

French Bingo –

These pages can be used to play French Bingo reenforcing your French vocabulary or, of course, just for fun.

Look on pages 13 - 29 and match these pictures with the correct sentences.

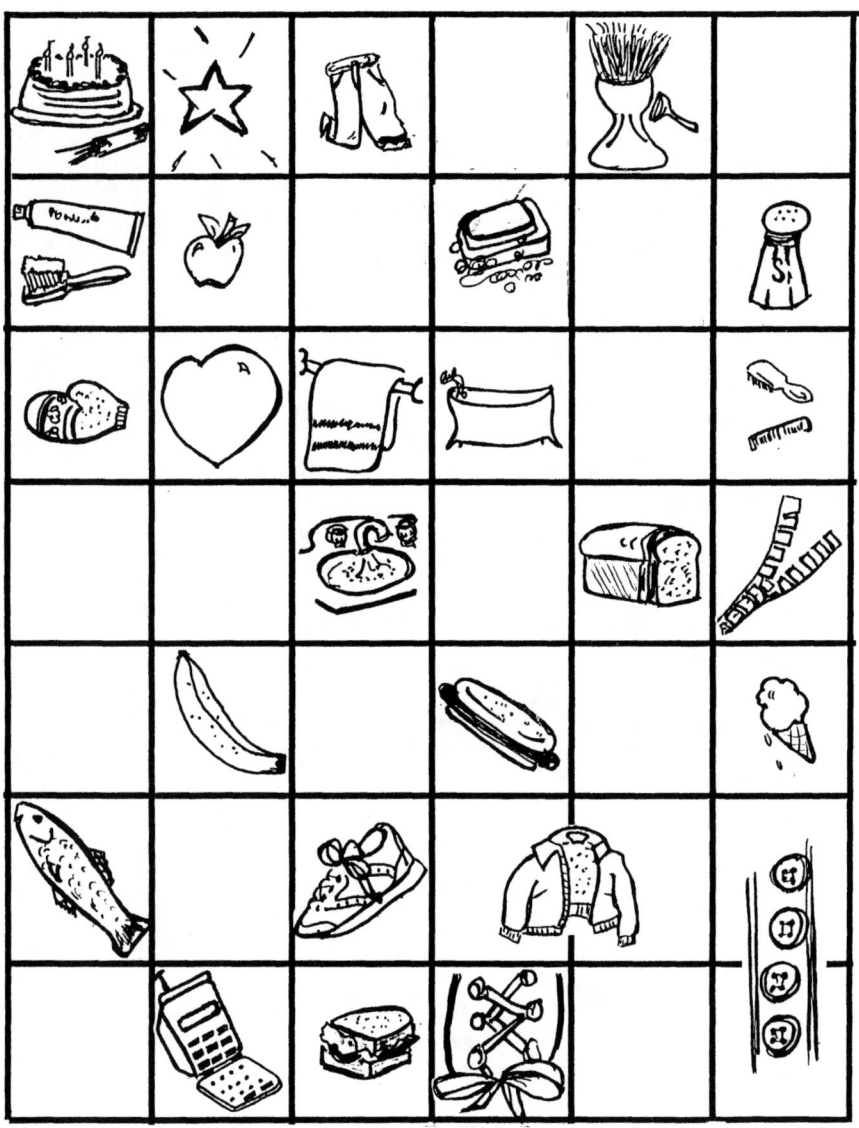

21   —   24   15   15

27   —   20   —   27   18

24   19   20   14   23

23   29   18

28   27   27

            24   23   28
23
            24   26   13

Look on pages 32 - 51 and match
these pictures with the correct sentences.

171

34   45   42   32

               42   32   35

40   35   42

46   40   34   43

50   34   41

51   40   37   51

33   43   —   51

Look on pages 53 - 77 and match
these pictures with the correct sentences.

173

55	76	61	—		57	58
70	75	57			66	58
	75		77	75	74	63
53	55	58		75	75	74
56		54		67	61	
						65
54		77			68	
70	62		55			75

Look on pages 78 - 119 and match these pictures with the correct sentences.

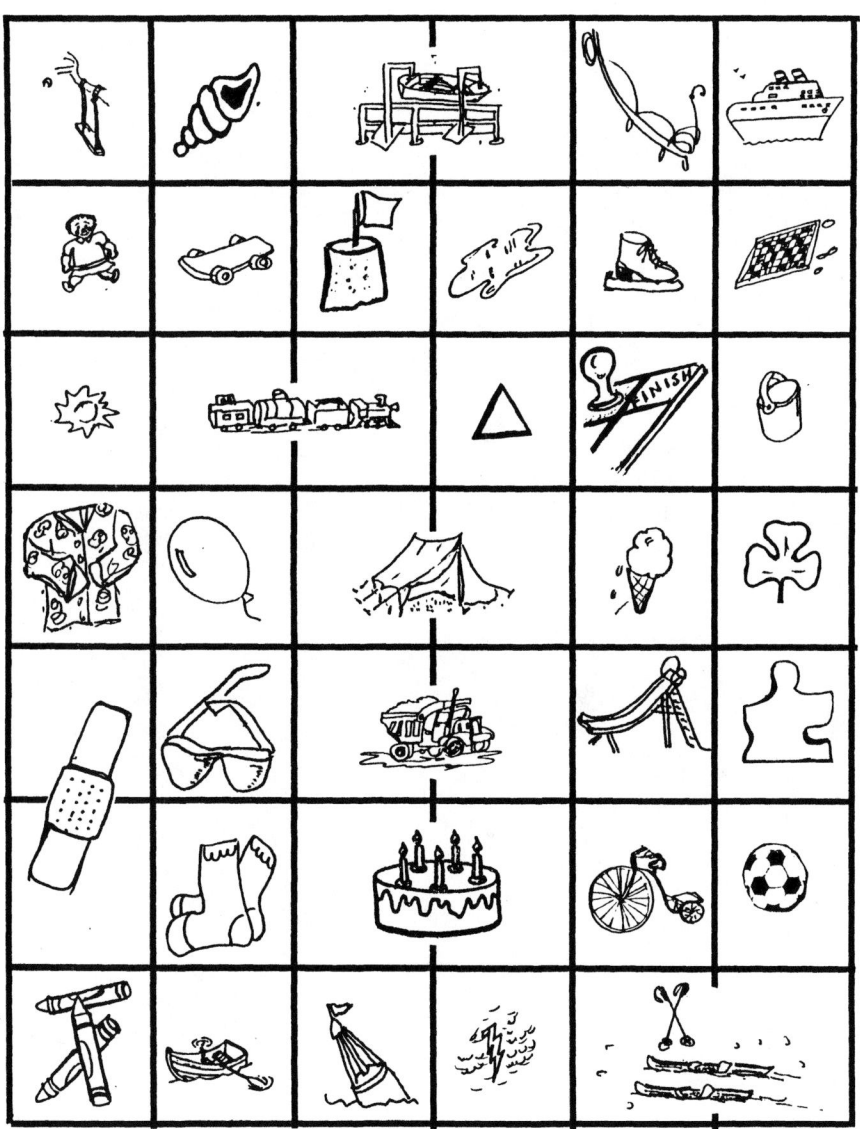

80	93		80		96	85
79	87	118	96		93	83
95	79	82		88		117
104	110		81		86	112
86	85		88		96	
						115
87	78		110		112	
	97		119	96	80	81